Brooklyn By Brushes

Written by Kevin Collins
Paintings by Michael Maggio, Sr.
and Students of his Art Classes

One Shot Productions (1-Shot Publishing)
Brooklyn, New York
Hampshire, England

A Children of the Night School Book
www.childrenofthenightschool.com
www.michaelspaintinginstructions.weebly.com

Cover image, "Brooklyn Bridge" by Michael Maggio, Sr., All Rights Reserved, July 2016.

For information on purchasing any of the original art shown in this book, other art by these artists, or commissioning an original art piece, please contact Michael's Painting Instructions at 718-925-5301, or via the website www.michaelspaintinginstructions.weebly.com or via email at Maggio124@aol.com.

ISBN-13: 978-1519232694
ISBN-10: 1519232691

All interior illustrations © by original artists, June 2016.

Interior Design by Kevin Collins

Printed in U.S.A.

Createspace

10 9 8 7 6 5 4 3 **2** 1   Second printing: March 2017

To the love of my life,
my wife of 55 years, Maria.
You have always been by
my side and I love you.

– *Michael Maggio, Sr.*
June, 2016

To my talented daughter,
Katie, for patiently learning
All the skills that Michael has
tried to impart to her.
And to my supportive wife,
Karen, for paying for
Katie's Art lessons.

– *Kevin Collins*
June, 2016

MICHAEL'S PAINTING INSTRUCTIONS FOR ADULTS AND CHILDREN
6 PARROT PLACE, BROOKLYN, NEW YORK 11228
(718) 925-5301 www.michaelspaintinginstructions.weebly.com

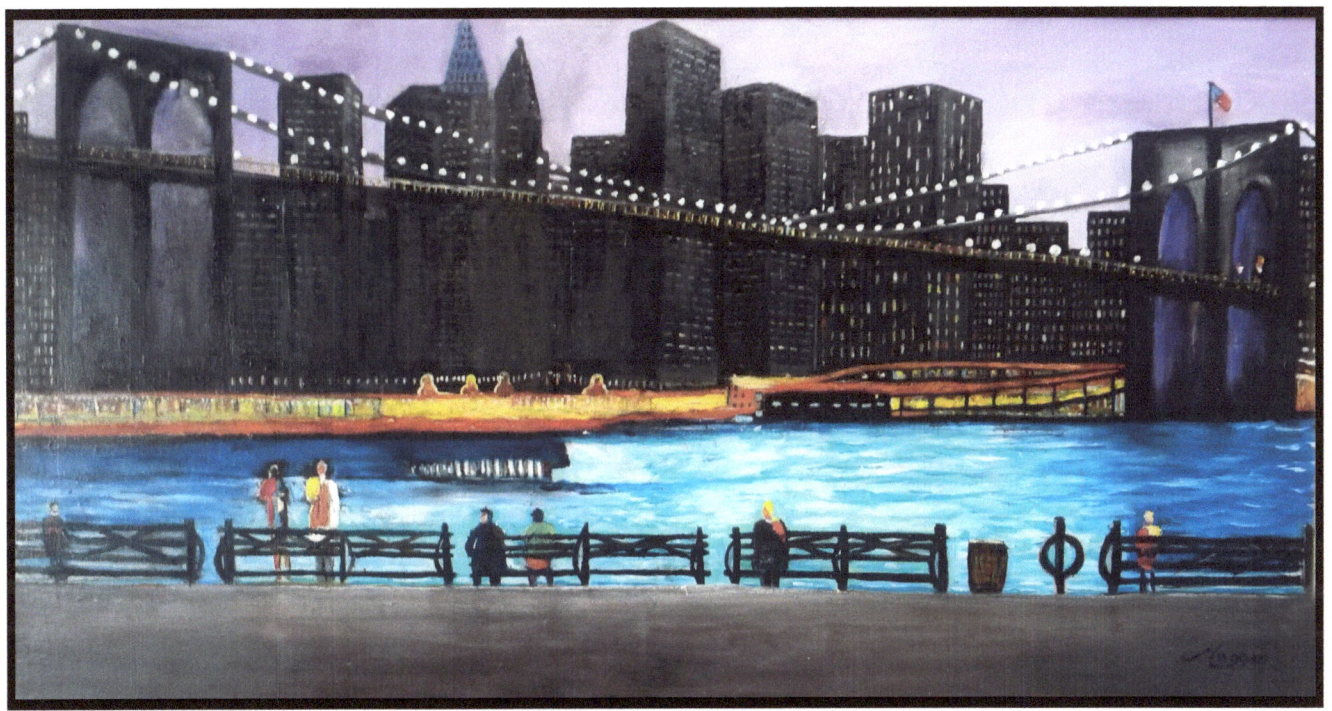

See Michael Maggio's expansive view of the Brooklyn Bridge in more detail on pages 7 - 8.

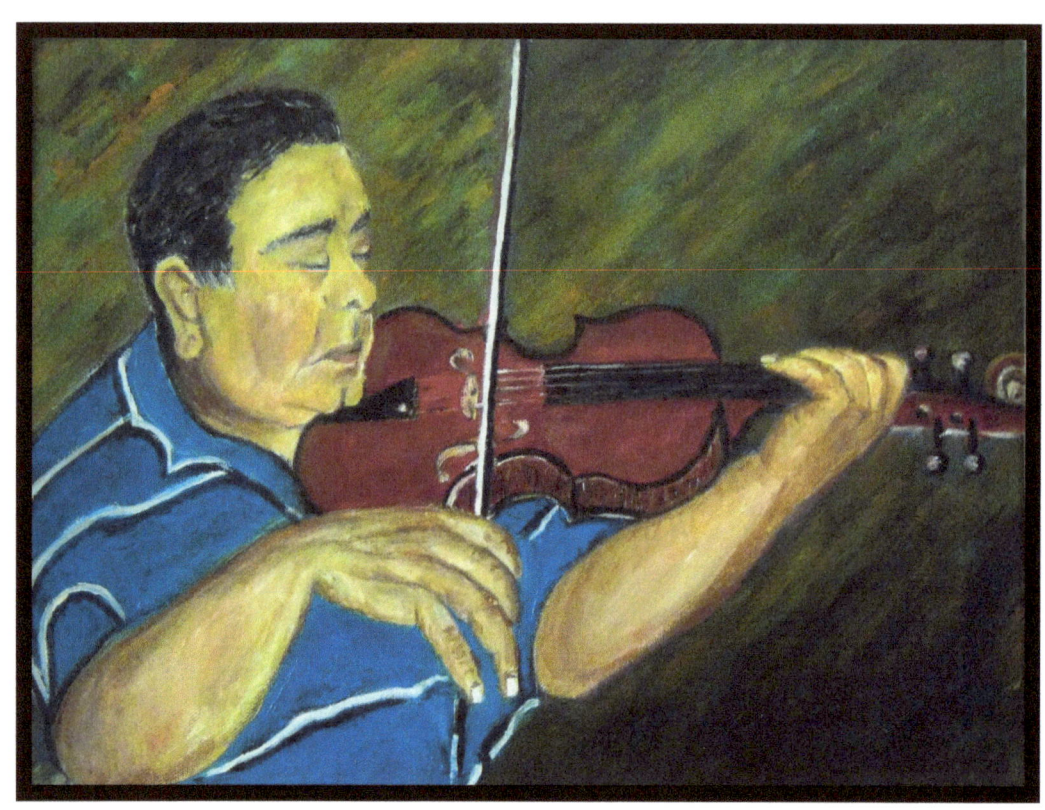

Michael Maggio, Sr. "Self Portrait" Oil on Canvas. 2000.

Introduction

I admit that this short book is primarily a vanity project, shamelessly showing off the high quality works of art created by Michael Maggio, Sr. and the students of his art classes.

My daughter began taking lessons from Michael in January, 2015, with no prior knowledge of how to put a brush to canvas and, in about 18 short months, she has shown a creative flourish and a desire to put her imagination on display for others to enjoy and appreciate.

None of this would have been possible without Michael's talent or his inexhaustible patience. Putting this book together is my feeble and wholly inadequate way of showing my appreciation of his talents, humility and generosity.

We decided to show off the talents of Michael and his students with a short study of Brooklyn, the best place in the world to live and experience life. We took a collection of art works created in these classes and we wanted to share them – along with other creations of these artists – with you.

We decided on a format that will feature some of the neighborhoods in our proud borough. What was amazing to us after trying to fit in so many of our students' paintings was that there was so many more that could have filled up a second book. Maybe someday that will happen.

Life without art is an incomplete existence. Perhaps if you will spend a few minutes with this book your life will be a bit more fulfilled than it was five minutes ago. If not, then at least you will still have the enjoyment of a brief vicarious visit to Brooklyn.

– Kevin Collins
June 2016

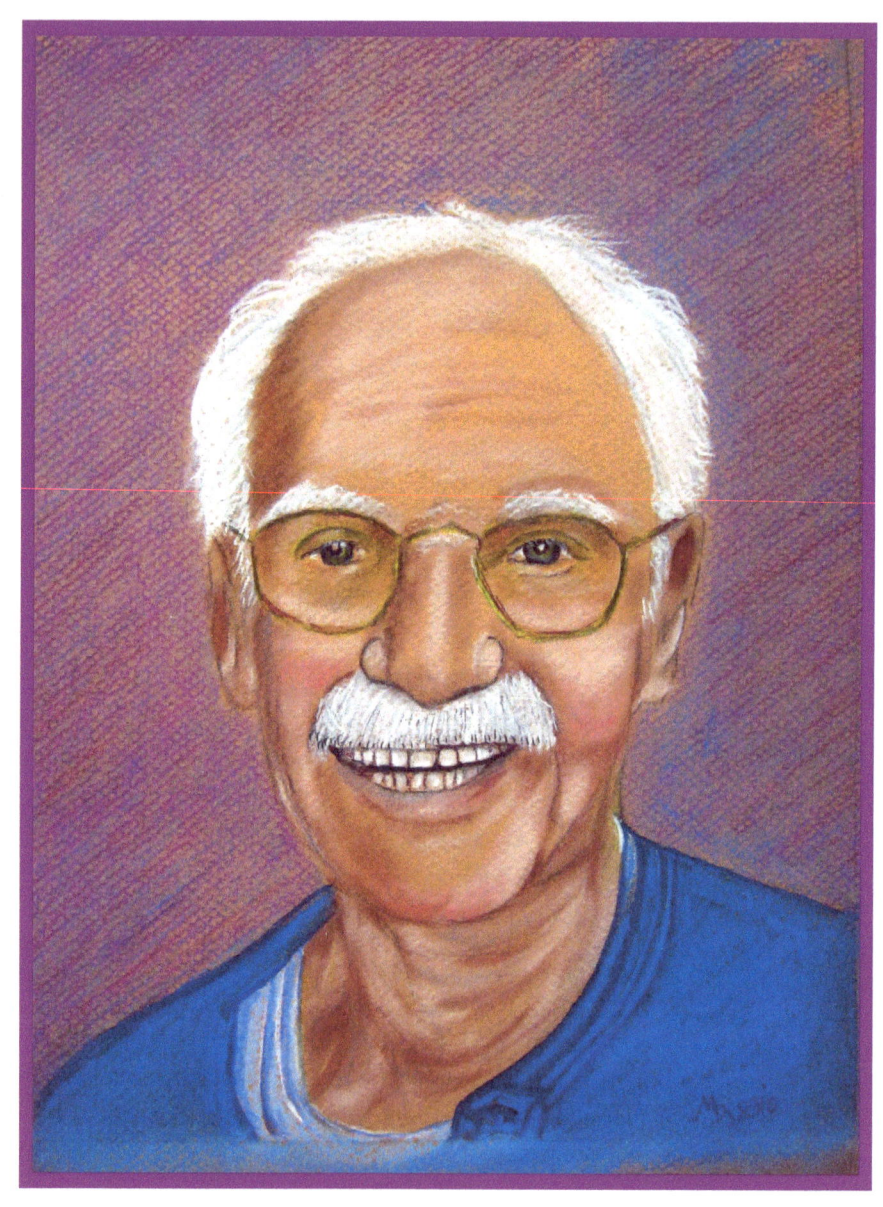

**For his inspiration and friendship, we remember
the late
WILLIAM SCHLIMMEYER
A student at Michael's. A student of the Arts**

Image by Michael Maggio, 8x10 in pastels

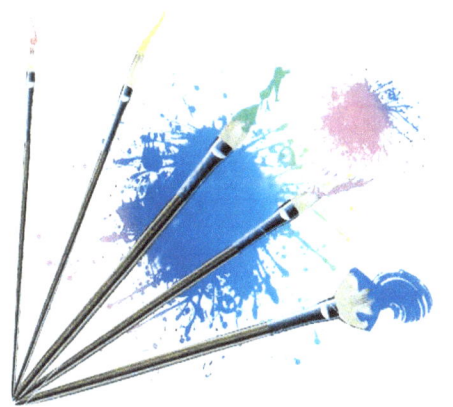

meet our instructor...

MICHAEL MAGGIO

Michael Maggio's journey to Brooklyn has been typically 20th Century Brooklynesque. As the hottest spot in this country's melting pot, Brooklyn has always been welcoming of new citizens from all over the world. Michael's family was settled in Sicily after the turn of the century but later moved to Tunis and then immigrated to the United States. It was on a return visit to Tunis when Michael was born in 1938.

Michael was truly a citizen of the world – well, at least a citizen of Europe – as he travelled through Italy and France where he eventually settled in Paris to study art and music.

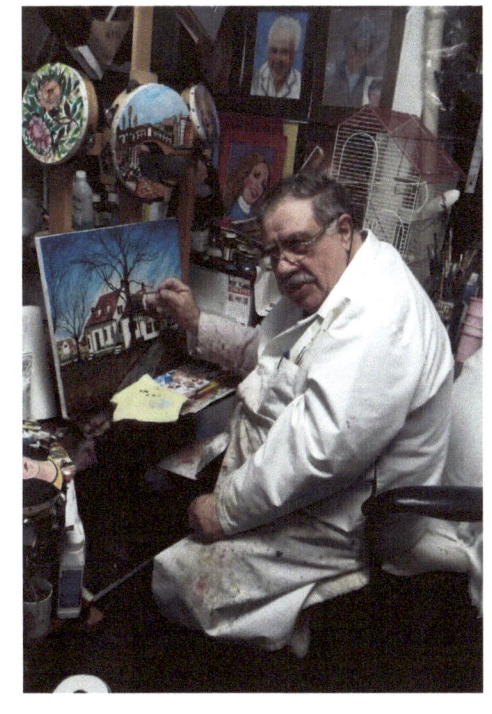

When his father's company moved to the United States in 1955, Michael came along and put down roots in Brooklyn. He was still honing his artistic and musical skills – showing particular talent on the piano and violin.

In time, military service came calling and Michael translated his musical knowledge to snare a relatively cushy position as a saxophone player in the U.S. Army Band based out of Fort Devens, Massachusetts. Asked by an assigning officer if any of the recruits could play the saxophone, Michael volunteered even though he had never touched the instrument in his life. Deft in the field, however, Michael quickly self taught himself the instrument and the military was none the wiser.

After his return to civilian life, Michael's talents grew and grew. His first attempt at putting paint to canvas was a picture of a little bird. Soon thereafter, he sold a painting of a Tuscany landscape to an Italian company. "It was a little 9x12 painting and they bought it for 20 francs because they said it looked like their grandmother's house back in Italy. It was only 20 francs but I felt like I had just won the lottery because I was finally a professional artist!"

As he developed his skills and turned them into a talent as an artist, Michael created two of his favorite paintings, "Napoleon Bonaparte" and "The Siesta". These two 24"x36" oil on canvas compositions received much praise and propelled Maggio to step up his efforts to hone his craft and to share his canvasses with others.

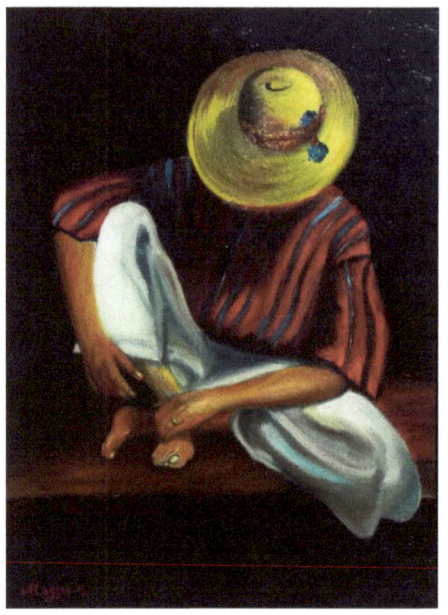

Ultimately finding himself at Rudy's Art School at 6 Parrot Place in Brooklyn in 1980, Michael was now learning the finer points of painting with oils. In 2000, when his master Rudy was ready to step down and retire, Michael stepped up and took over the school. He's been there ever since.

Michael has a simple and honest incentive to teach painting: he just wants newcomers, young and old, to try their hands at the canvas. He often muses, "Even if you don't think you have the talent, the time or the money, try it just once...you might like it. If you want to be an artist, first you should learn all about drawing – shapes and colors – and have a lot of patience to keep doing things over and over again until you succeed!"

Success is not measured by how many paintings you sell but how much pleasure the art of painting brings to you.

Michael's Private Painting Instructions is now well established as a long standing icon of Bay Ridge. Ensconced on tiny Parrot Place (a brief off-shoot of Seventh Avenue), the studio is sat directly across the street from the beautiful Dyker Golf Course and Dyker

Dog Run, the tiny studio feeds the creativity of students from ages 6 to 96. Students can choose their once-a-week preferred class time from afternoons to evenings five days a week. Michael charges a small monthly fee, looking not to turn a profit but to inspire and share. "I'm not doing this to make a fortune," he'll frequently say, "I'm here to make friends and to share the love of art."

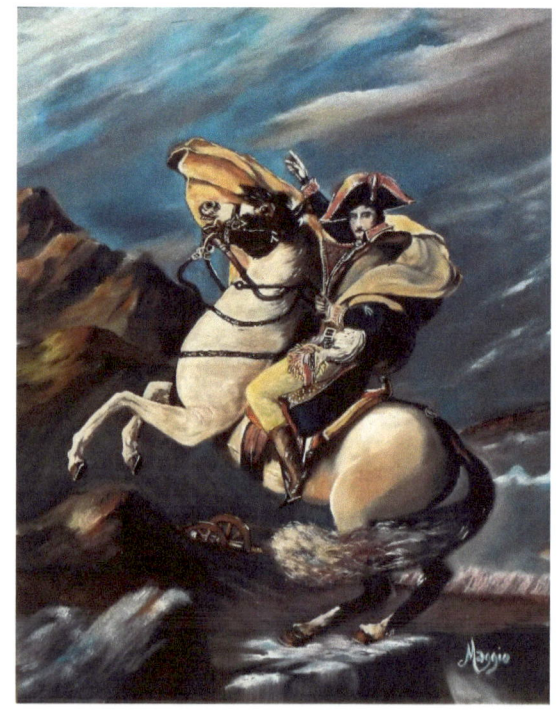

What is it that fuels Michael's long love affair with Brooklyn? Food in general. Canolis in particular.

It is Michael's love of the Borough of Kings that inspired this little collection of artwork. What better way for him to give back to Brooklyn than to reflect on some of the people, places, sites and attractions that have breathed life into the town over the centuries?

And so, Brooklyn by Brushes...

Brooklyn GRAND ARMY PLAZA

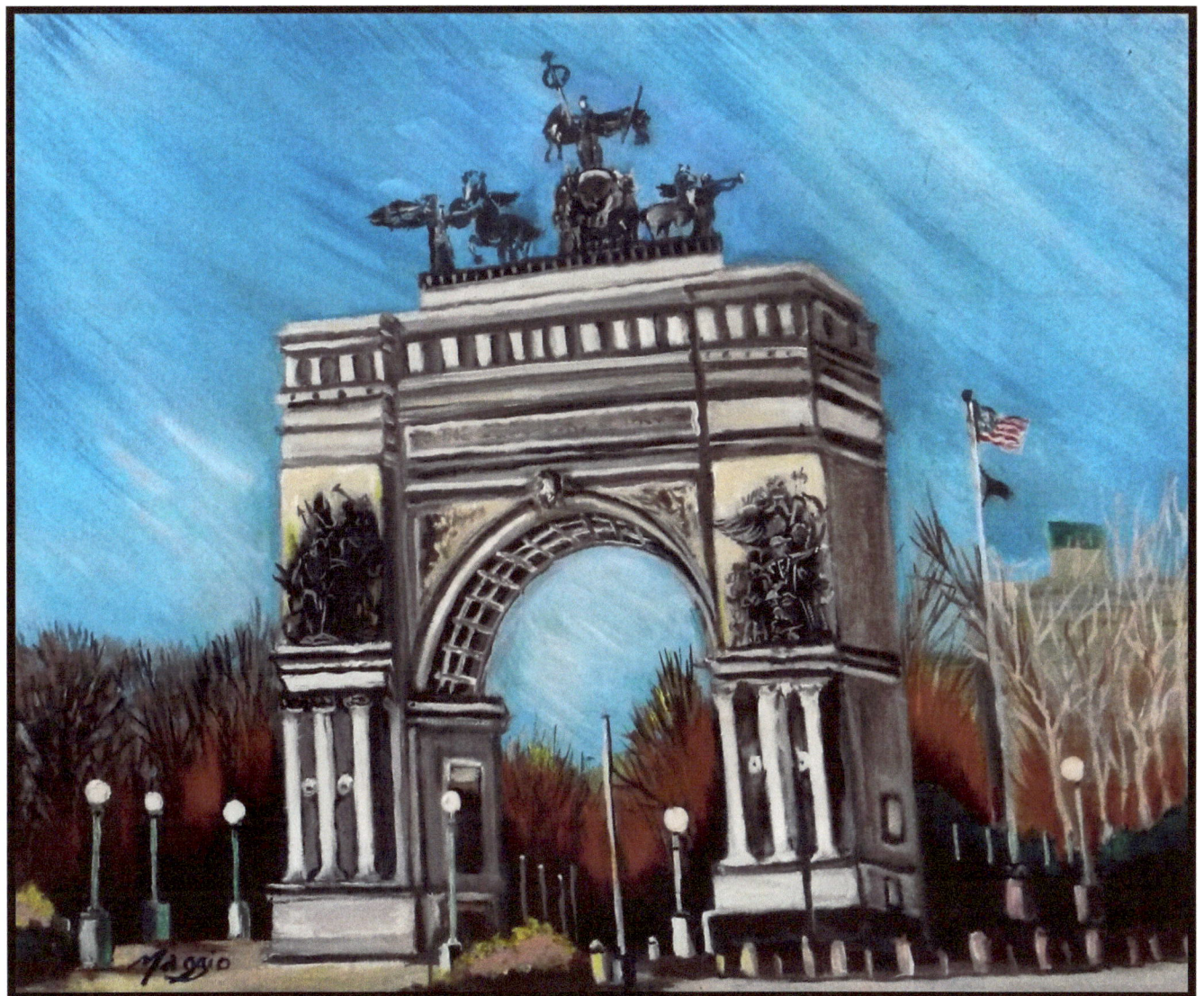

MEMORIAL ARCH by Michael Maggio

The **Memorial Arch,** also known as the Soldiers' and Sailors' Arch", looms 80 feet tall over Grand Army Plaza, just off the entrance to Prospect Park. The monument was completed in 1892 as a triumphal arch dedicated "To the Defenders of the Union, 1861-1865". It has a stairway to an observation deck and a portion of its interior is sometimes opened for art shows and performances.

The striking 16"x20" oil on canvas by **Michael Maggio** captures the pride and majesty of the structure that dominates the landscape at the end of Eastern Parkway.

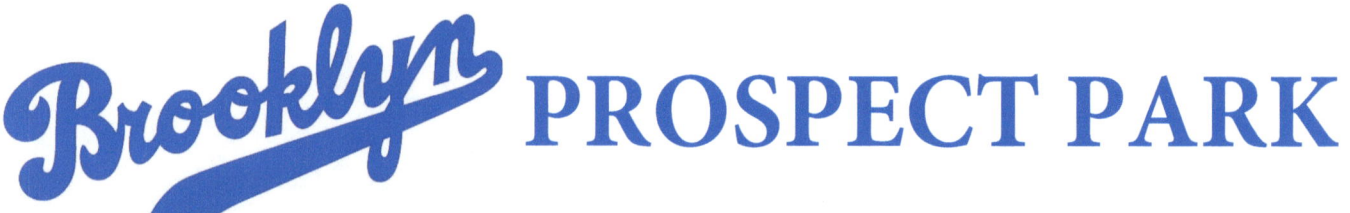

Brooklyn PROSPECT PARK

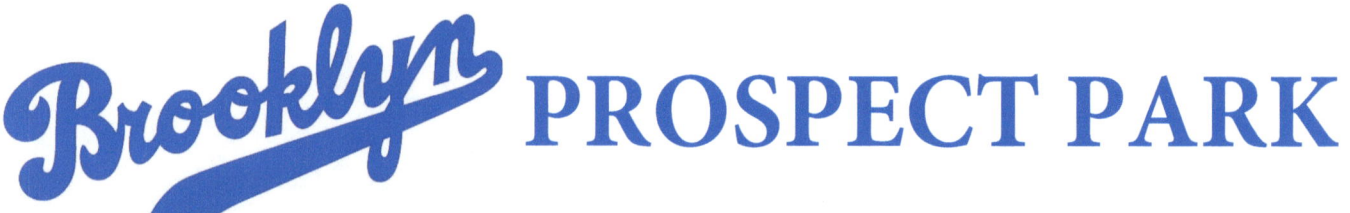

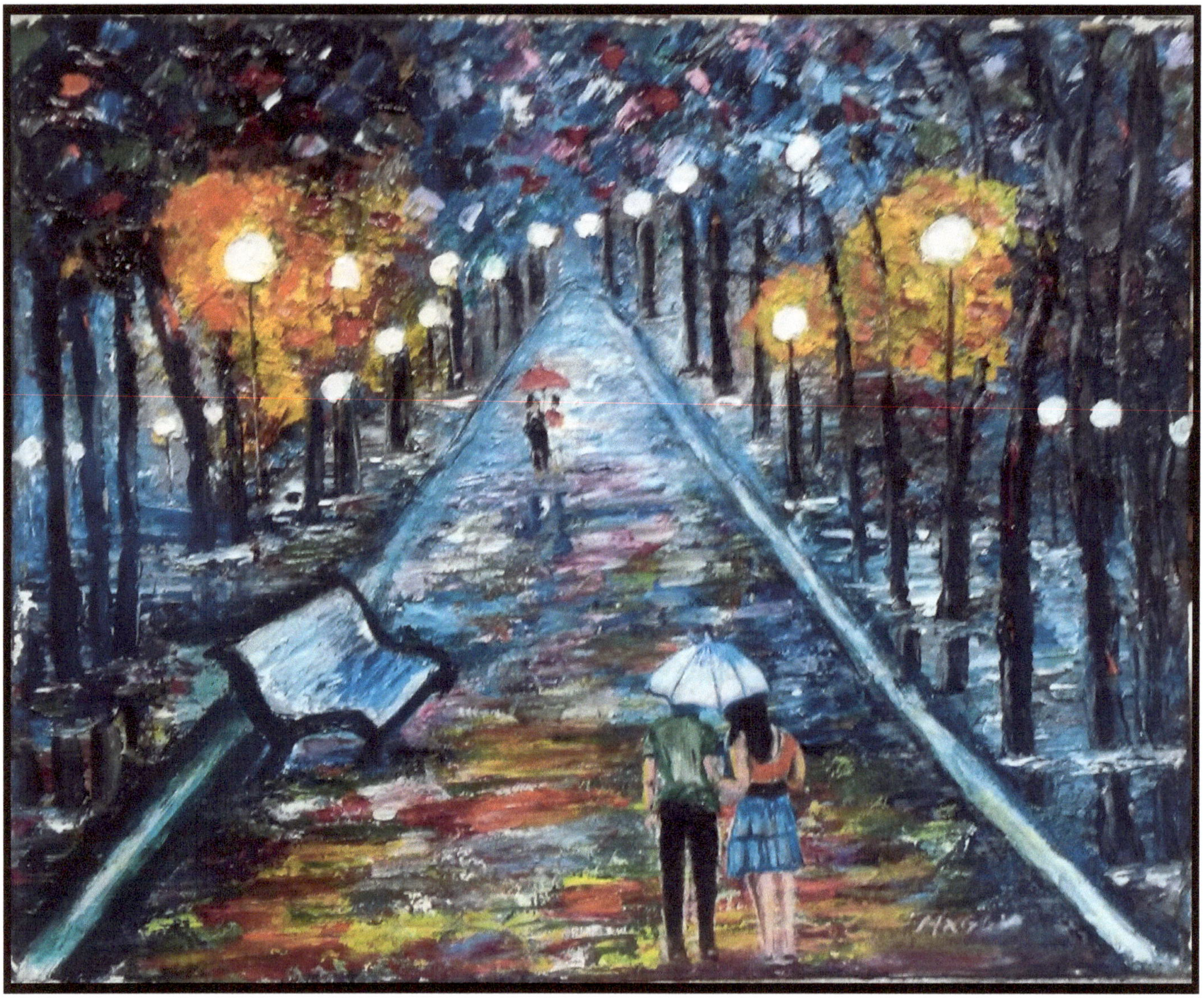

PROSPECT PARK BY NIGHT by Michael Maggio

Prospect Park is Brooklyn's proud answer to Manhattan's (slightly) more famous Central Park. It was created in 1867 and is visited by more than 8-million people every year. The verdant grasses run up against Brooklyn's only lake, a boathouse, a nature conservancy, a skating rink, the Prospect Park Zoo and the grave of Montgomery Clift. The park has gone through many ups and downs but, at its best, is a bit of rural respite in the heart of a big city.

Michael Maggio 's imaginative depiction of couples strolling through the park under the shine of street lamps encapsules the romantic ideal of the park. The image was created in oil using palette knives on an 11"x14" canvas.

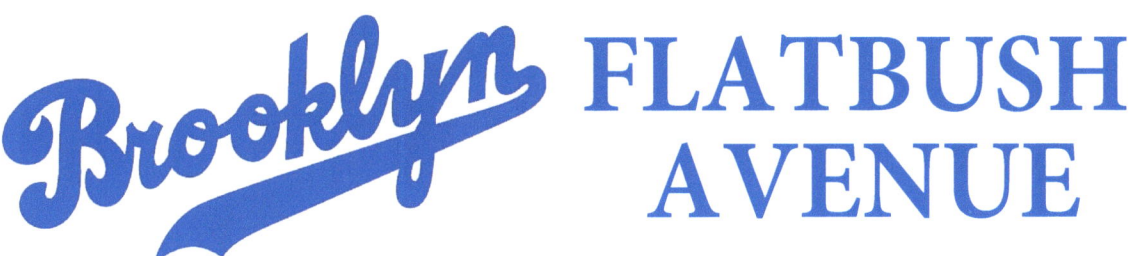

Brooklyn FLATBUSH AVENUE

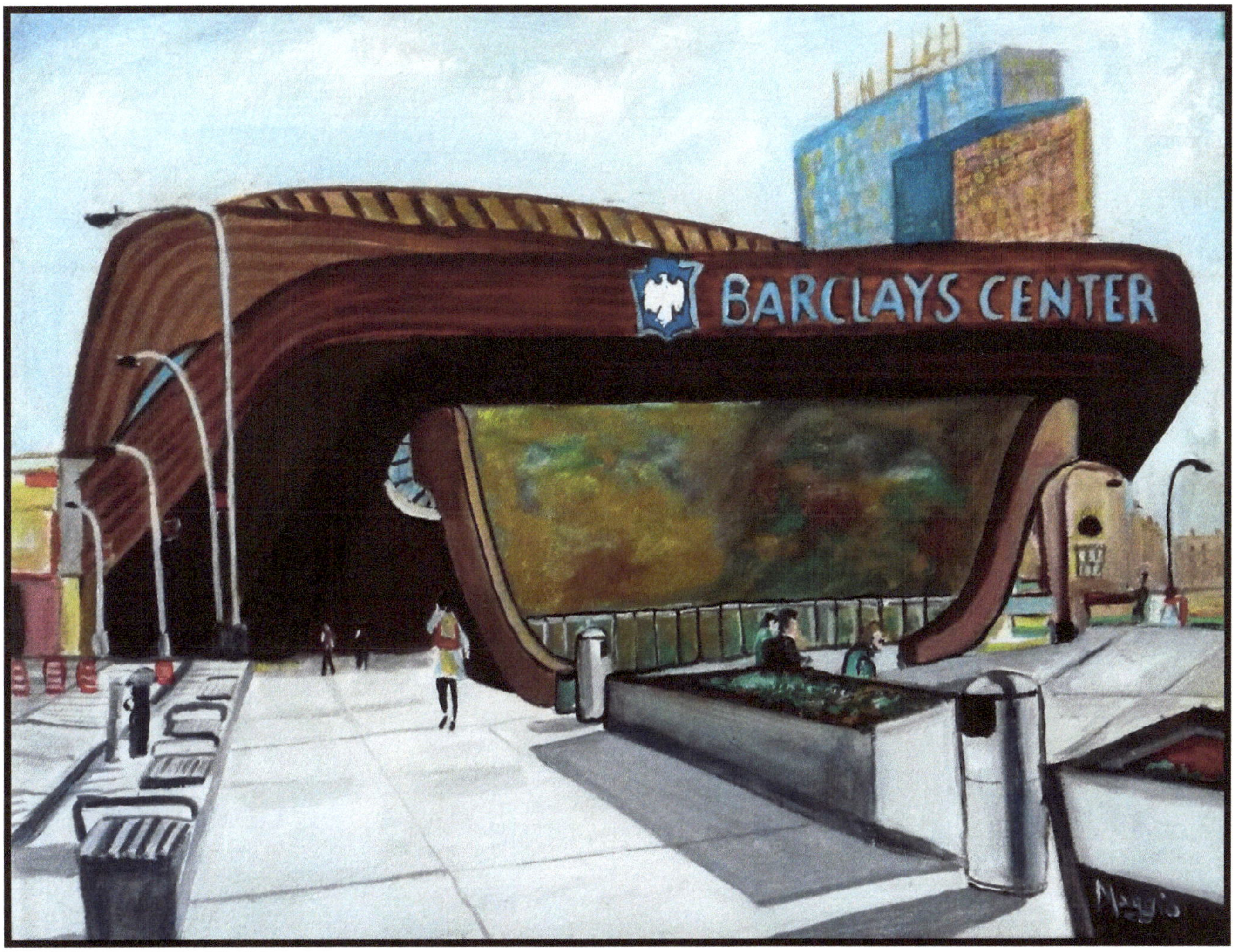

BARCLAYS CENTER by Michael Maggio

Attempting to revitalize its downtown neighborhoods, Brooklyn was proud to open up the multi-purpose Barclays Center arena on the northern end of Flatbush Avenue in 2012. The spectacularly odd-shaped venue features a sloping design with excellent seating for all events. It is now the home of the *New York Nets* of the National Basketball Association and the *New York Islanders* of the National Hockey League. The arena has also become a frequent home for the *Ringling Brothers and Barnum and Bailey Circus* when the troupe visits Brooklyn.

Capturing a view of the northern ediface, with the grass covered information booth barely concealing our view of the structure's stunning "oculus" skyview, **Michael Maggio** depicts, in oil, an inviting view of the spectacular and welcoming entrance to the city's crown jewel arena. The original is on 12"x16" canvas.

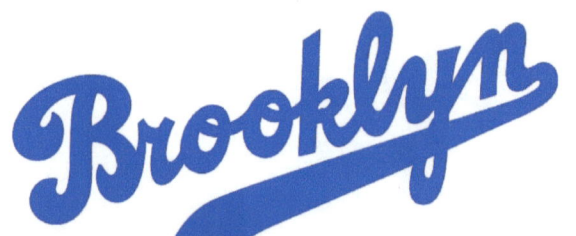
THE BROOKLYN BRIDGE by Michael Maggio

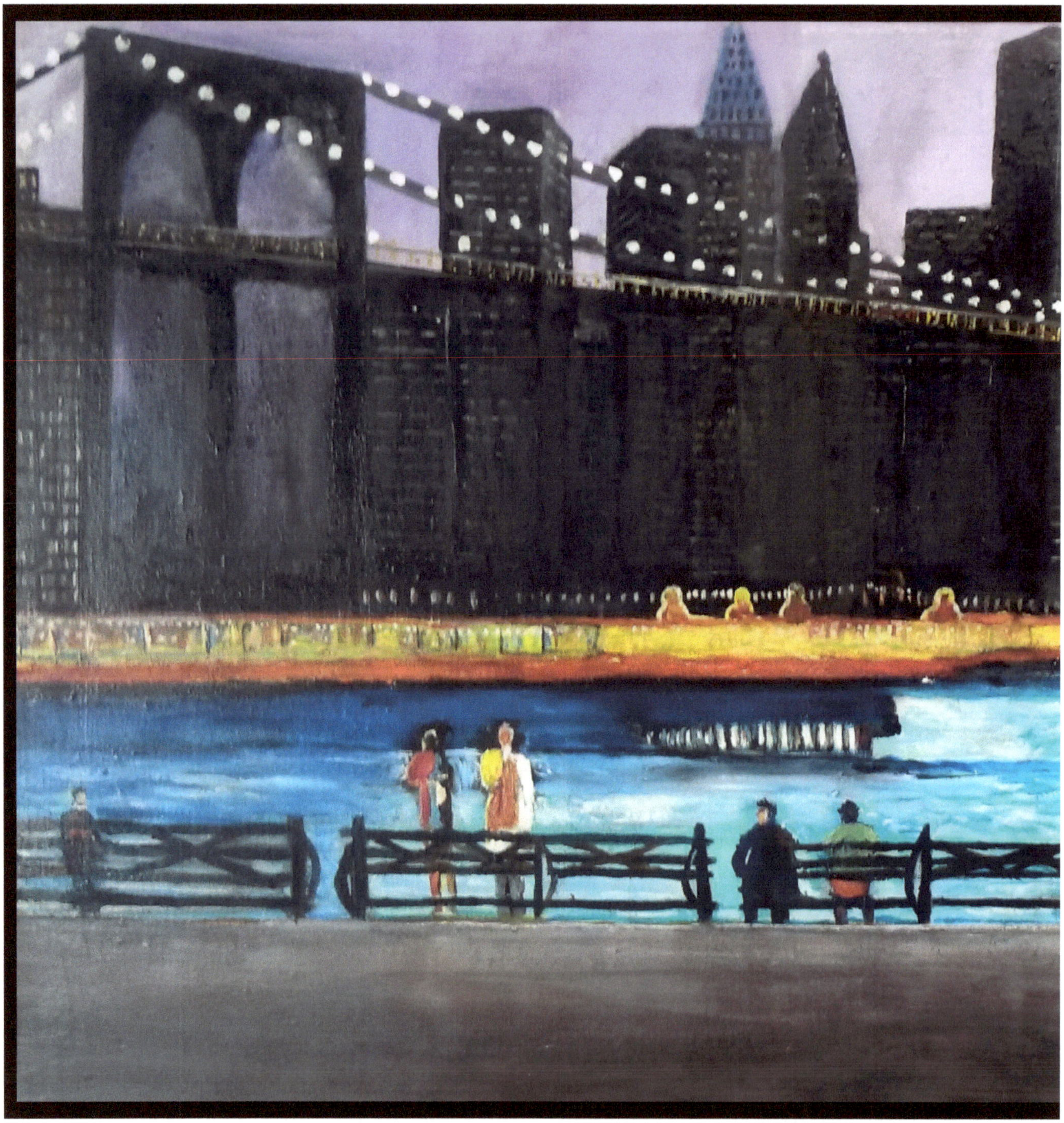

A National Historic landmark since 1964, the Brooklyn Bridge is 1,595.5 feet of history and legend. Connecting Brooklyn with Manhattan, the iconic span opened in 1883 and has firmly settled into the American zeitgeist ever since. It has been home to daredevils' death defying stunts, magnificent fireworks displays, and a parade of elephants led by the world's most famous showman, P.T. Barnum.

You've seen it in movies, television shows and read about it in books and magazines. It is quite literally the grand entrance to Brooklyn. Just beware of anyone trying to sell it to you.

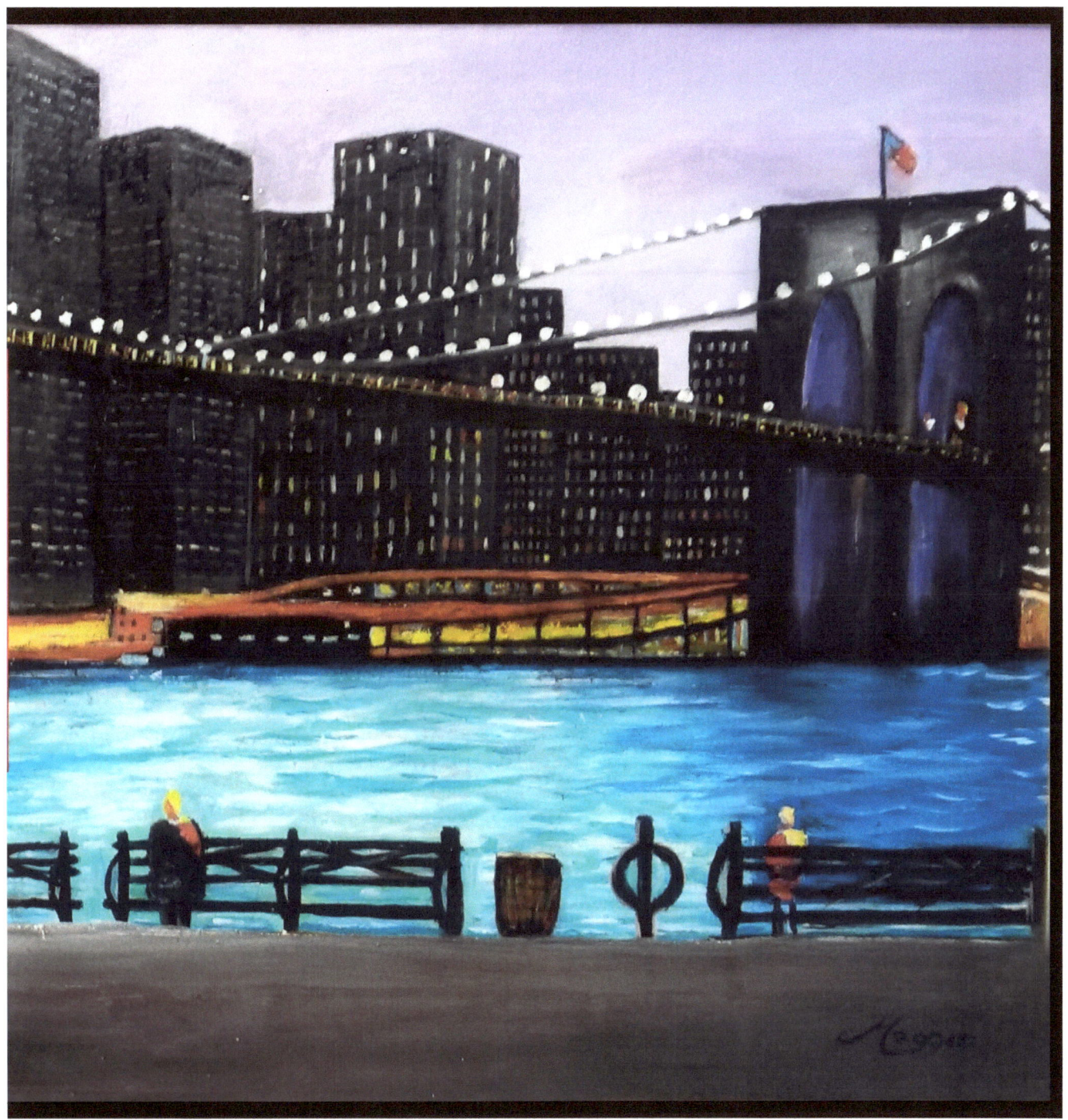

This view of the bridge from the nearly-as-famous Brooklyn Heights Promenade shows off the glamour of the span and the glistening waters of the East River. This sumptuous oil on canvas is a spectacular 18"x36" and is currently featured in the front window of Michael's Painting Instructions Studio.

Brooklyn CONEY ISLAND

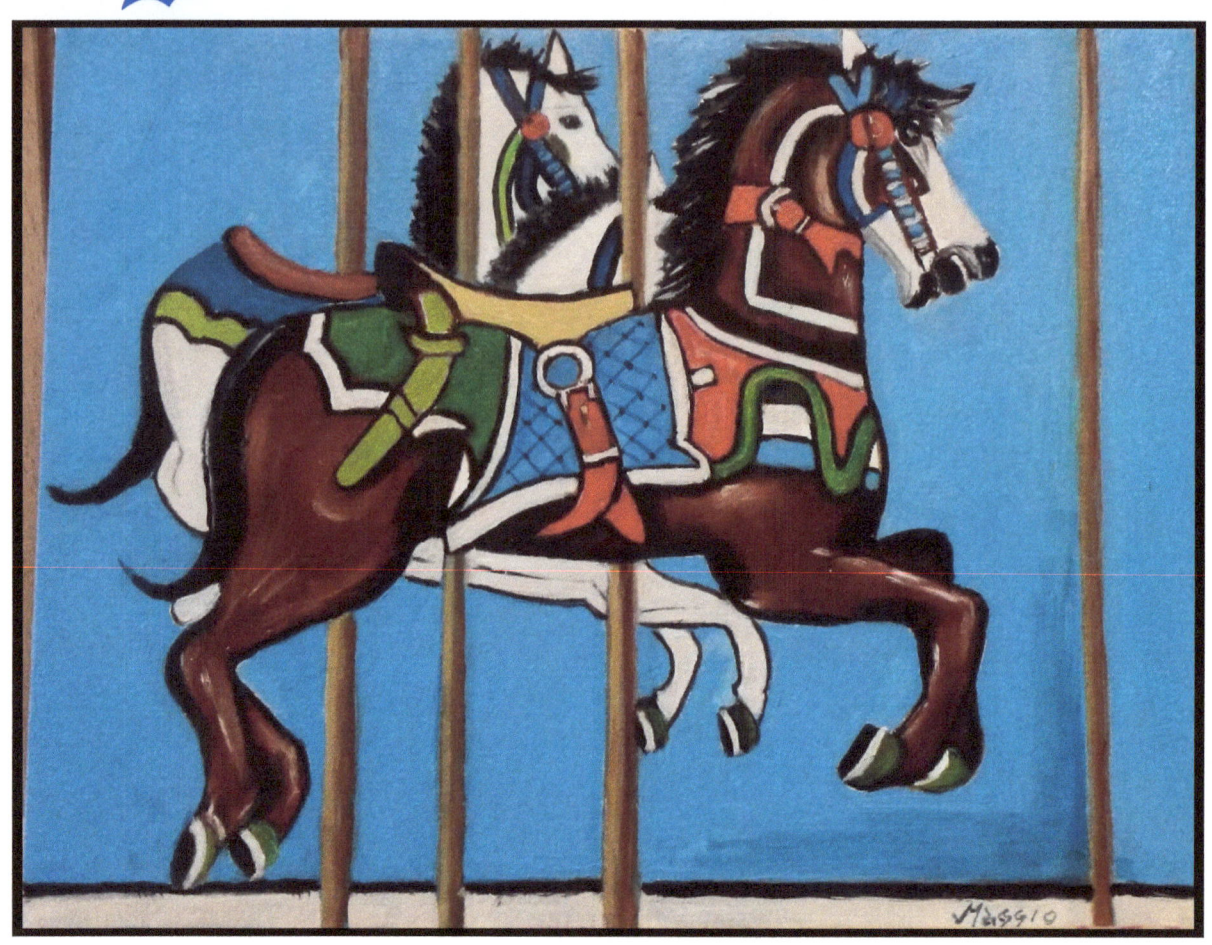

CONEY ISLAND CAROUSEL by Michael Maggio

Does any other site scream "Brooklyn!" more than Coney Island? From shortly after the Civil War up through the World War II era, Coney Island – which is now actually a man-made peninsula along the southwestern shore of Brooklyn – was the home of the largest amusement park in the entire United States. Coney Island's boardwalk, beach front, bright lights and innovations have been replicated and reproduced in amusement parks worldwide. Consisting of a cavalcade of historic theme parks such as Luna Park, Steeplechase Park and Dreamland, Coney Island continues to attract many millions of fun-seekers every year.

From the time the first wooden carousel was constructed and opened in 1876 until right up to the present day, Coney Island is the destination on the east coast for the ultimate "real" amusement park adventure. Its carousels have become legendary.

Michael Maggio's 12"x16" **Coney Island Carousel Horses** was painted from one of his many memories of the park with many merry-go-rounds. This should remind many a Brooklynite of bright summer days and long summer nights going 'round in circles at the world's premiere entertainment park.

8

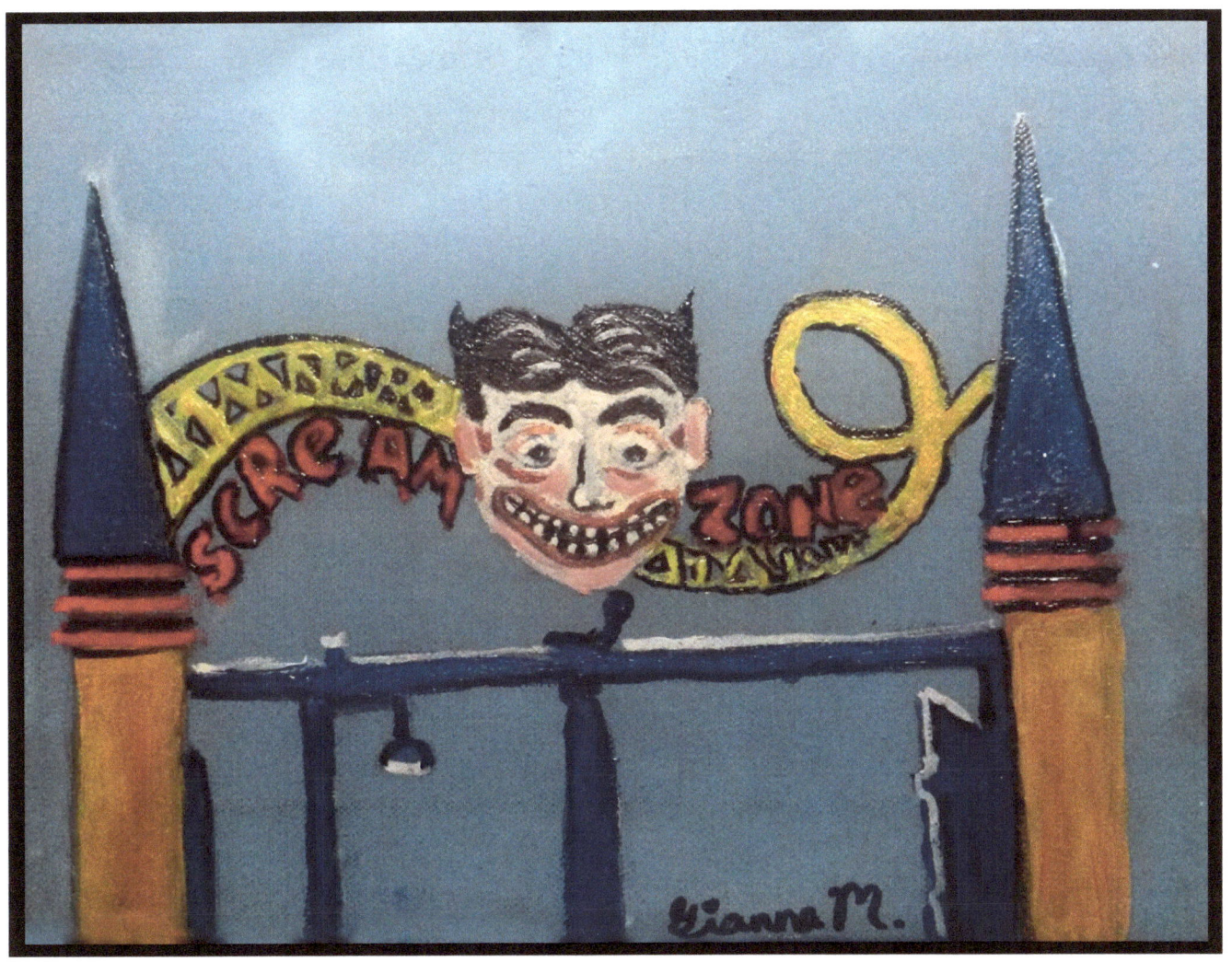

SCREAM ZONE by Gianna Maggio

Tillie the Clown's intriguingly odd smiling face welcomed throngs of millions to **Steeplechase Park** in Coney Island for many of the latter years of the park. The park lured customers onto its rides and into its amusements from 1897 through 1963. Park goers entered the gates under the weird gaze of Tillie – named for park founder George C. Tilyou – but, admittedly, hardly anybody used that name: the Joker-ish imp was most affectionately known as the "Funny Face". In the park's early years the original version of the face would wink from above the front gate at entrants who were about to buy their daily tickets. In its last decade or so, the modern "Funny Face" was more stoic but still sent gleeful shivers of fear and anticipation up and down the spines of millions of children who weren't quite sure whether amusement or bemusement lay in wait for them in the fun zone on the other side of the gates.

11-year old **Gianna Maggio** put oil to canvas to create this 8x10 depiction of the brand new Scream Zone featuring the funny face that Steeplechase visitors cherish today.

Coney Island has a proud history of iconic rides that are well known throughout the world and have established the park as the iconic amusement arena of all time.

The clickety-clackety wooden roller coaster known as **The Cyclone** has frightened the hot dogs out of riders for nearly 90 years.

"Brooklyn's Eiffel Tower", the 250 foot tall **Parachute Jump** is now defunct but can still be seen from miles away as you travel up and down Brooklyn's southern shore has either caused or cured a fear of heights in intrepid jumpers from 1941 until it closed in 1964.

The **Wonder Wheel**, located in Deno's Wonder Wheel Amusement Park, holds 24 passenger cars and looms 150 feet above the park. Possibly the most well-known Ferris wheel in the world (London's Eye? Fuhgeddaboudit!) Legend holds that Wonder Wheel has been stopped only one time during park hours since it opened in 1920 and that was during the infamous massive New York City blackout in 1977.

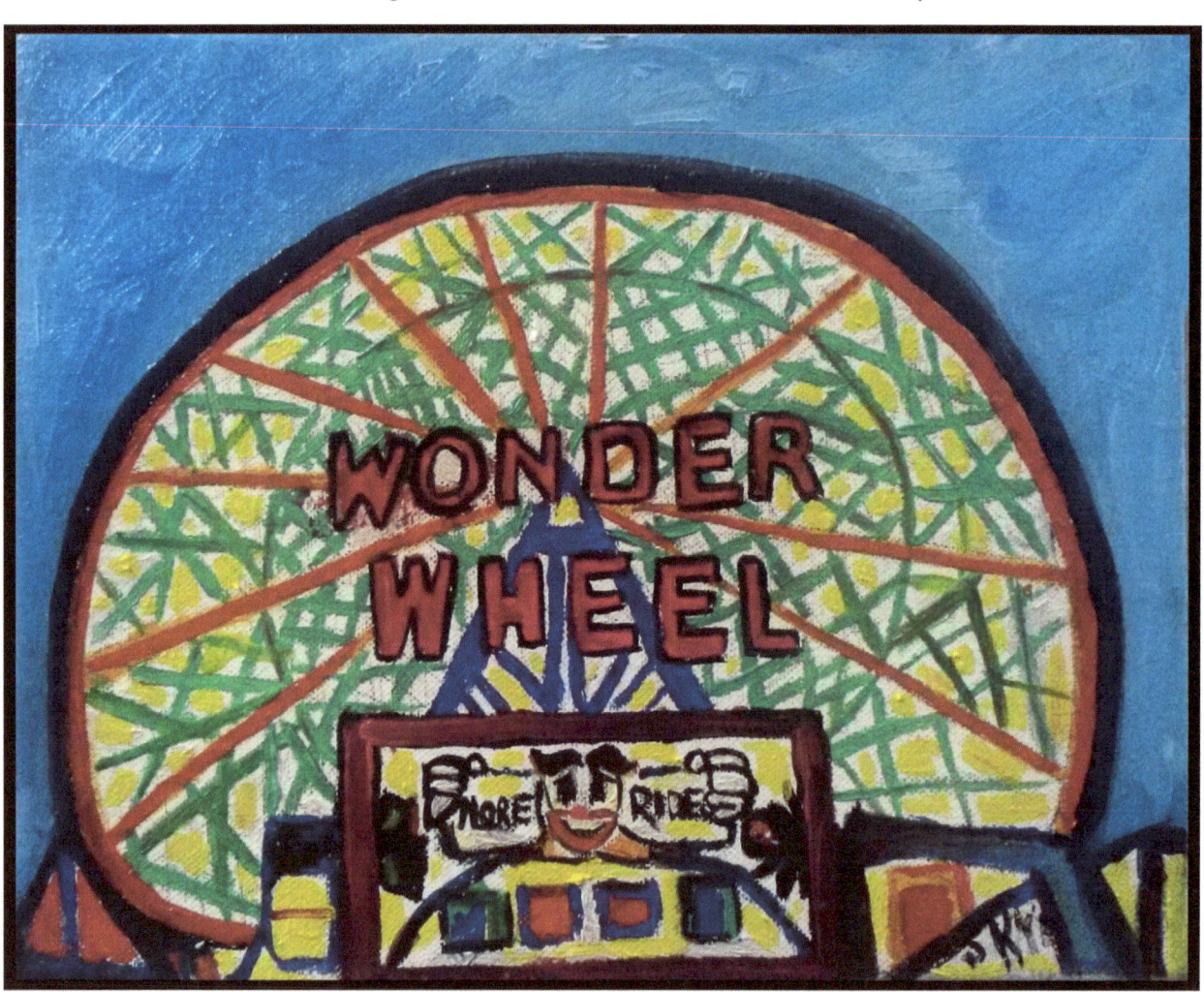

WONDER WHEEL by Skye Bleu

11-year old **Skye Bleu** imagined Wonder Wheel in oil on a 9"x12" canvas and in a slightly impressionistic style. Its bright colors, endless array of lights, enormous signage and classic clown are all memorable components of the Ferris wheel that runs circles around all other Ferris wheels.

A fixture on Surf Avenue for these past 100 years, **Nathan's** is famous for its signature hot dogs, crinkle-cut French fries, Philly Cheese Steaks and hamburgers. Founded by Polish immigrants Nathan and Ida Handwerker in 1916, Nathans has become synonymous with Coney Island and its pure beef hot dogs have become the epitome of fine seaside eating.

Brooklyn legend suggests that while working at Feltman's German Gardens (a popular Coney Island restaurant at the time), Nathan and Ida got the idea to start their own competing business from a pair of singing waiters named Jimmy Durante and Eddie Cantor. They opened their nickel hot dog stand and the rest is history.

Fun Facts: FDR once served Nathan's hot dogs to visiting royalty. The first 4th of July Nathan's Hot Dog Eating Contest was in 1916 -- it has been held every year since 1972. Nathan's on Surf Avenue has been open virtually continuously for 100 years since 1916 with closings only due to 2012's Hurricane Sandy and a small fire the following year.

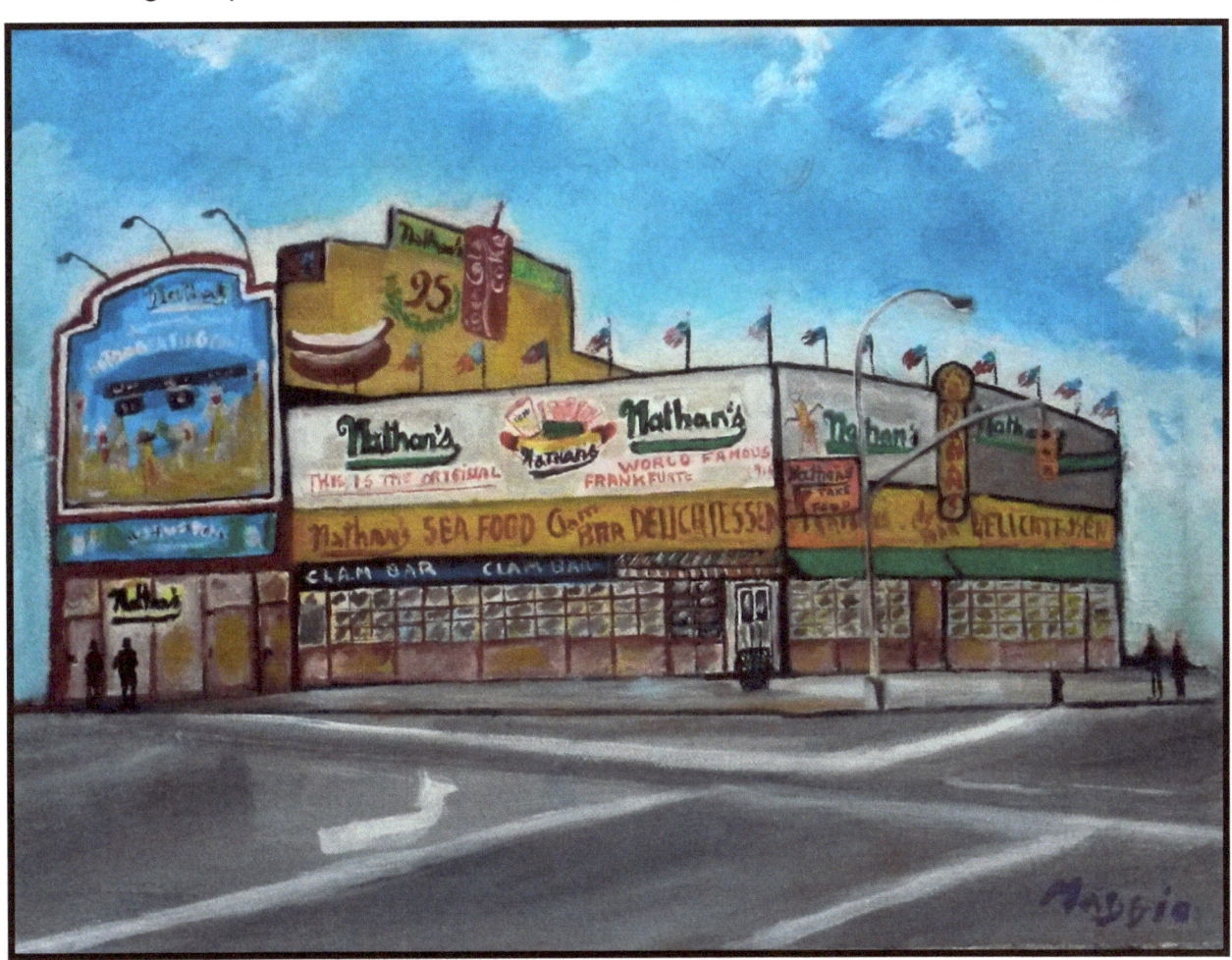

NATHAN'S FAMOUS by Michael Maggio

Nathan's never looked as delicious as it does in this oil depiction by **Michael Maggio** on 12"x16" canvas. Painted in 2016 but showing the restaurant as it stood in 2011 (rumor has it that the yellows in the image may actually include a hint of mustard).

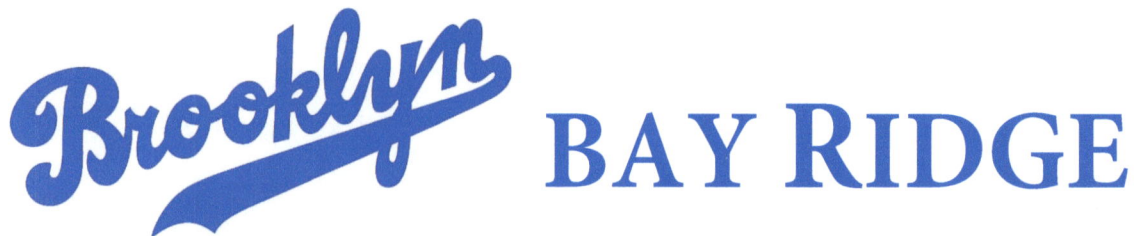

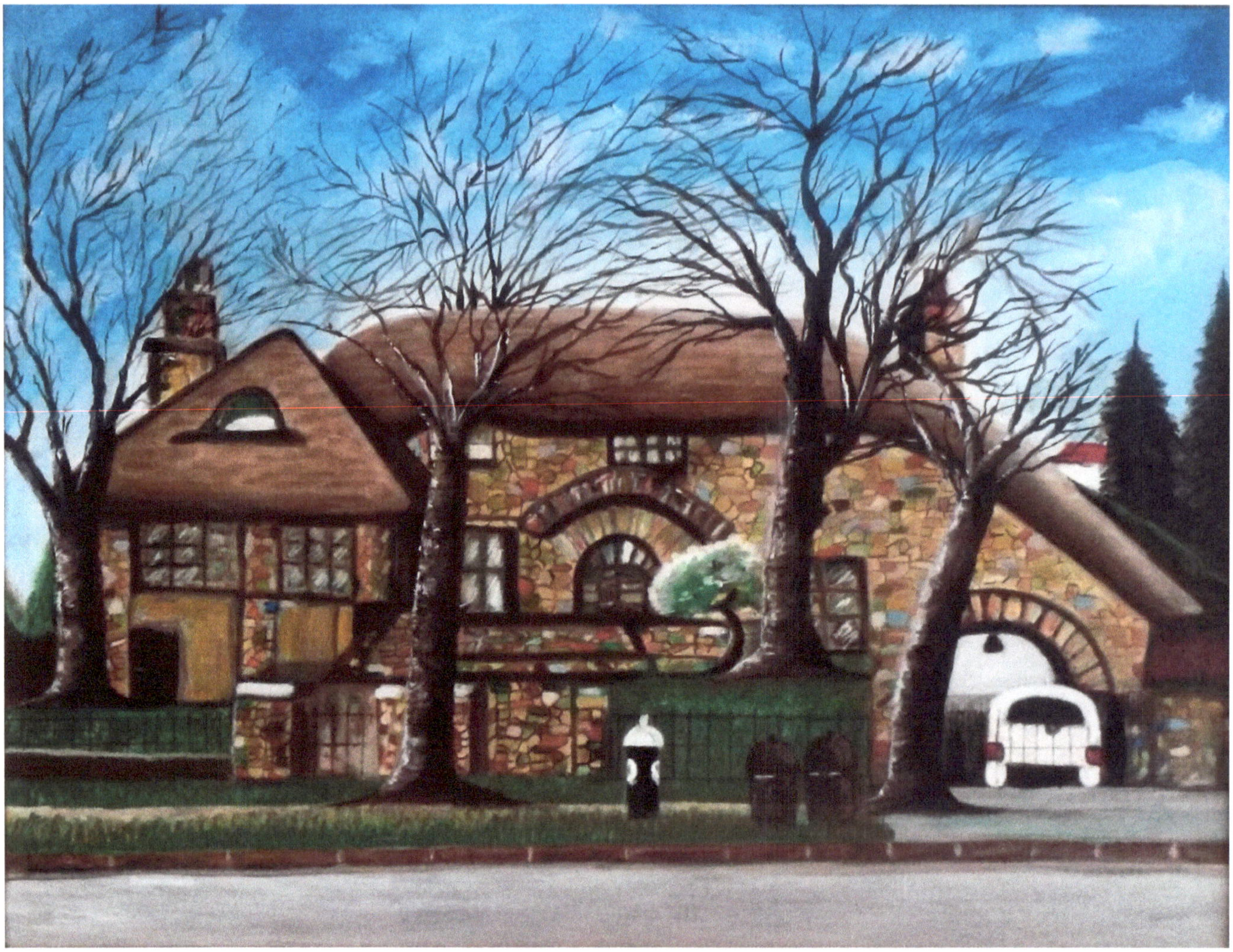

THE GINGERBREAD HOUSE by Michael Maggio

Brooklyn has been popularized on screens small and large as a continuous series of houses either attached or semi-attached with their key feature being neverending and redundant rows of stoops. Not so! Brooklyn has a wide variety of curious and exceptional architecture and its homes reflect the diversity of incomes and interests of their builders and owners. The memorable Gingerbread House was constructed in 1917 and boasts stained glass, iron gates, beamed ceilings, thatched roof and stone walls. In recent years it was put on the market for a tidy asking price of 11-million dollars.

Michael Maggio captured the rustic splendor of the first building in Bay Ridge to be designated as an historic landmark with its eye-popping copper and brown hues. The 18"x24" oil on canvas proves that Brooklyn has a bit of fairyland at its roots.

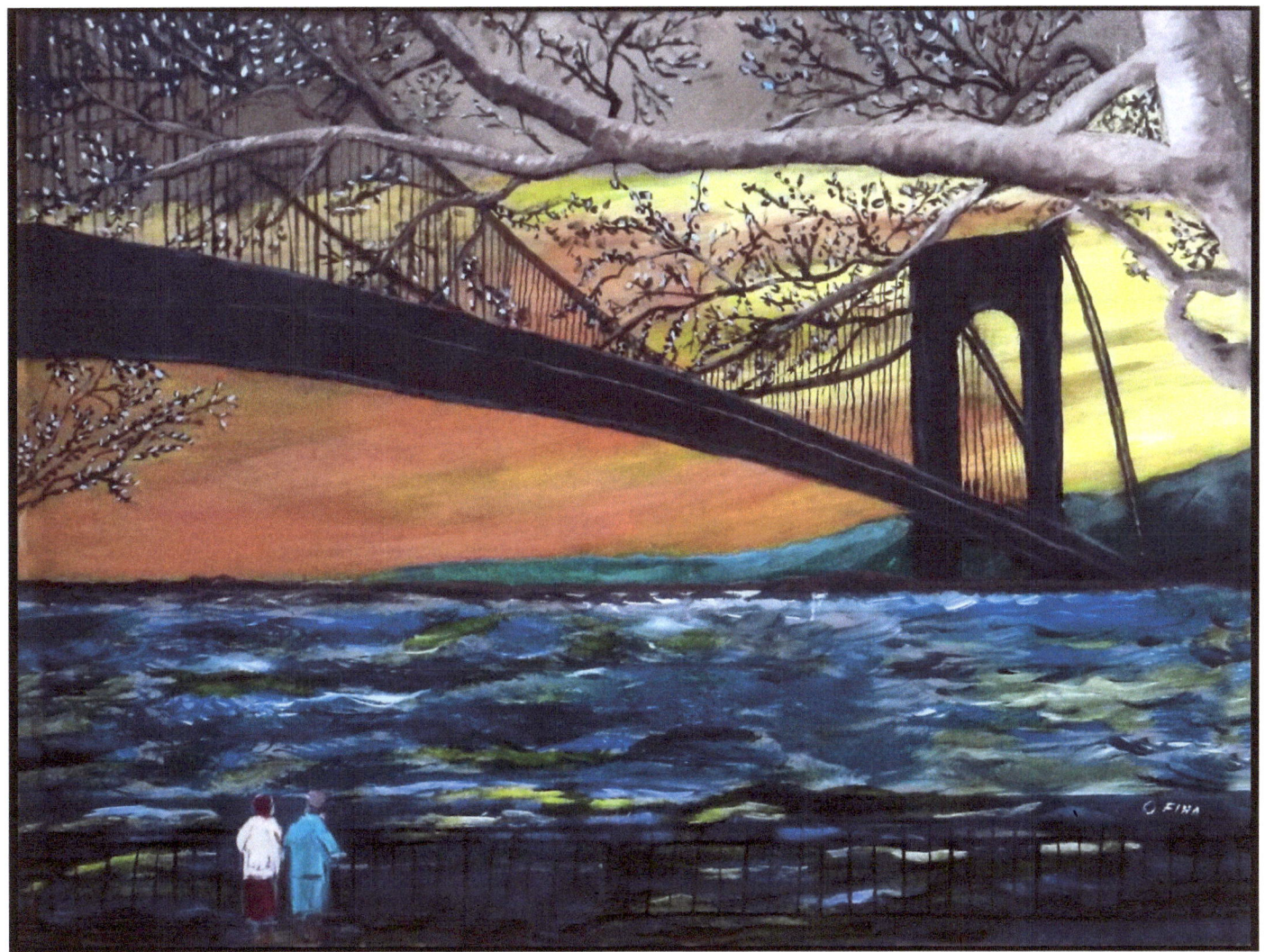

VERRAZANO-NARROWS BRIDGE by Vinny Fina

Okay, we know the bridge's name is spelled wrong, but a strong grasp of spelling and grammar has never been a strong suit when speaking Brooklynese. Linking Brooklyn to Staten Island since 1964, the **Verrazano** (we hardly ever add the "Narrows" part) is still America's longest suspension bridge at 4,298 feet. Popularized in American culture, the bridge features prominently in many movies such as 'Annie Hall', "Saturday Night Fever', 'Prince of the City', 'The Abyss', 'Tree of Life' and 'The Avengers'.

Vinny Fina caught the Verrazano on a blustery fall day with the sun descending and the water chopping down the Narrows. Vinny is one of the studio's longest and most productive students. His oil on canvas version of the Verrazano measures in at 24"x36".

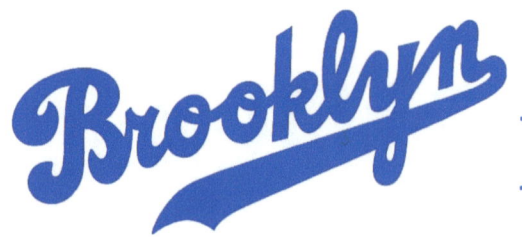 **BENSONHURST**

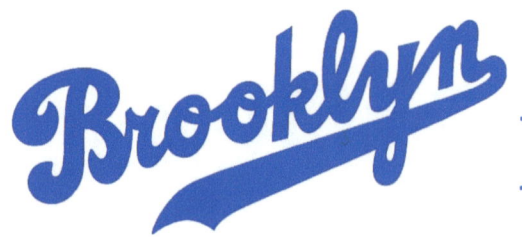

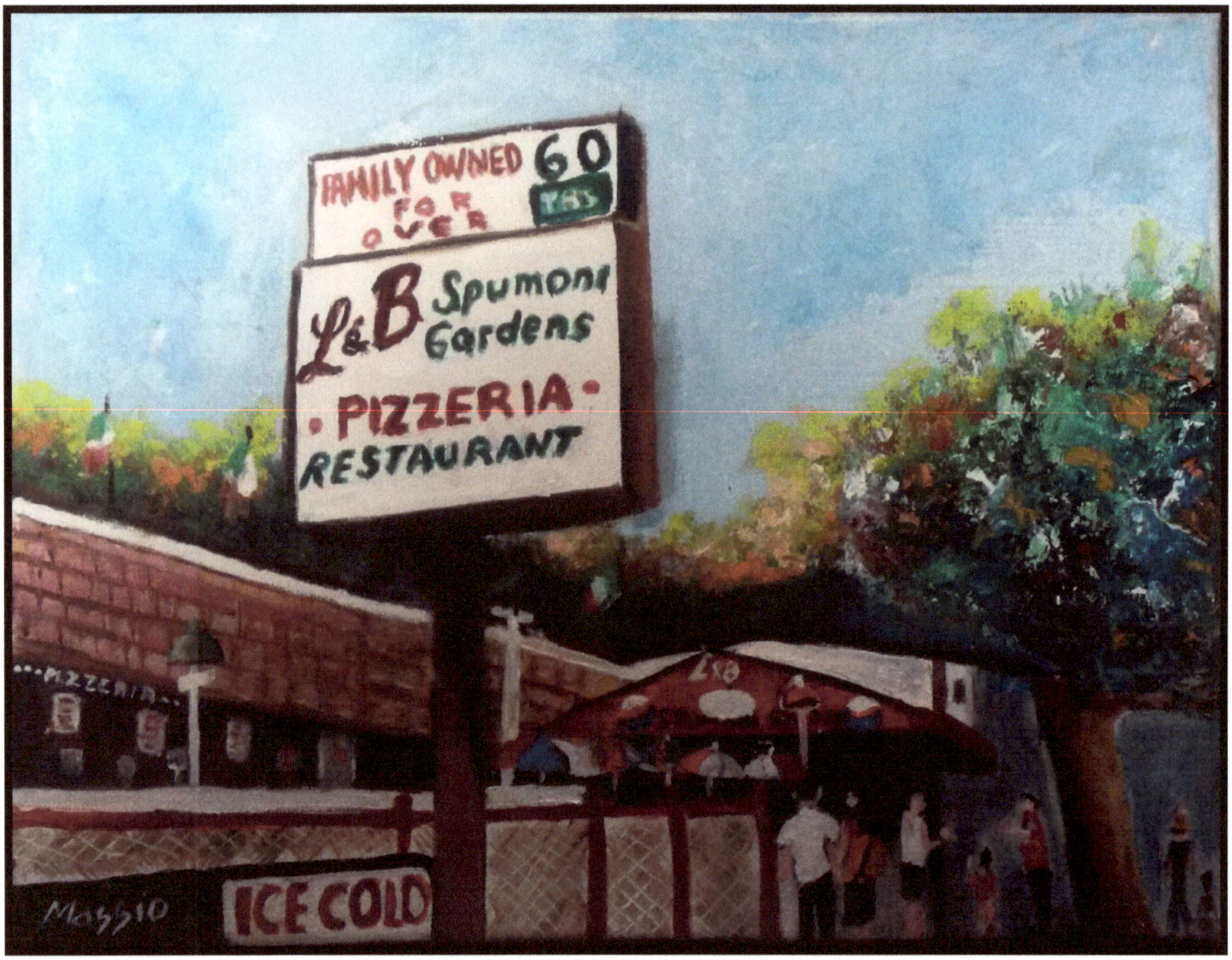

L&B SPUMONI GARDENS by Michael Maggio

If Brooklyn has been famous as a melting pot for people, it has even further cemented its melting pot reputation when it comes to food. Wildly popular in Bensonhurst -- and to visitors from all over the world -- is **L&B Spumoni Gardens** on 86th Street.

Locals and visitors frequent the gardens for its scrumptious resturant fare and its round and Sicilian pizza, spumoni, tiramisu and Italian ices. Come in and sit down or just order from the walk-up window.

In this mouth watering 12"x16" oil on canvas **Michael Maggio** invites hungry art lovers to one of the most highly praised Italian eateries on the East Coast.

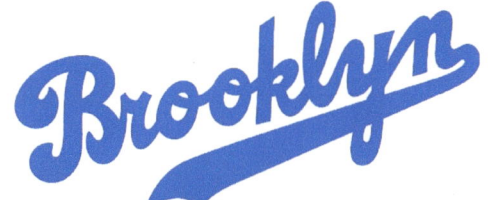

BENSONHURST

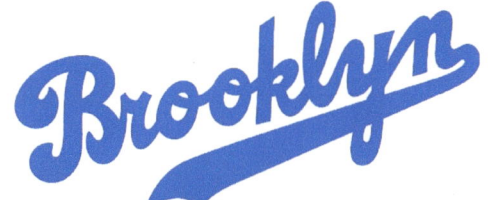

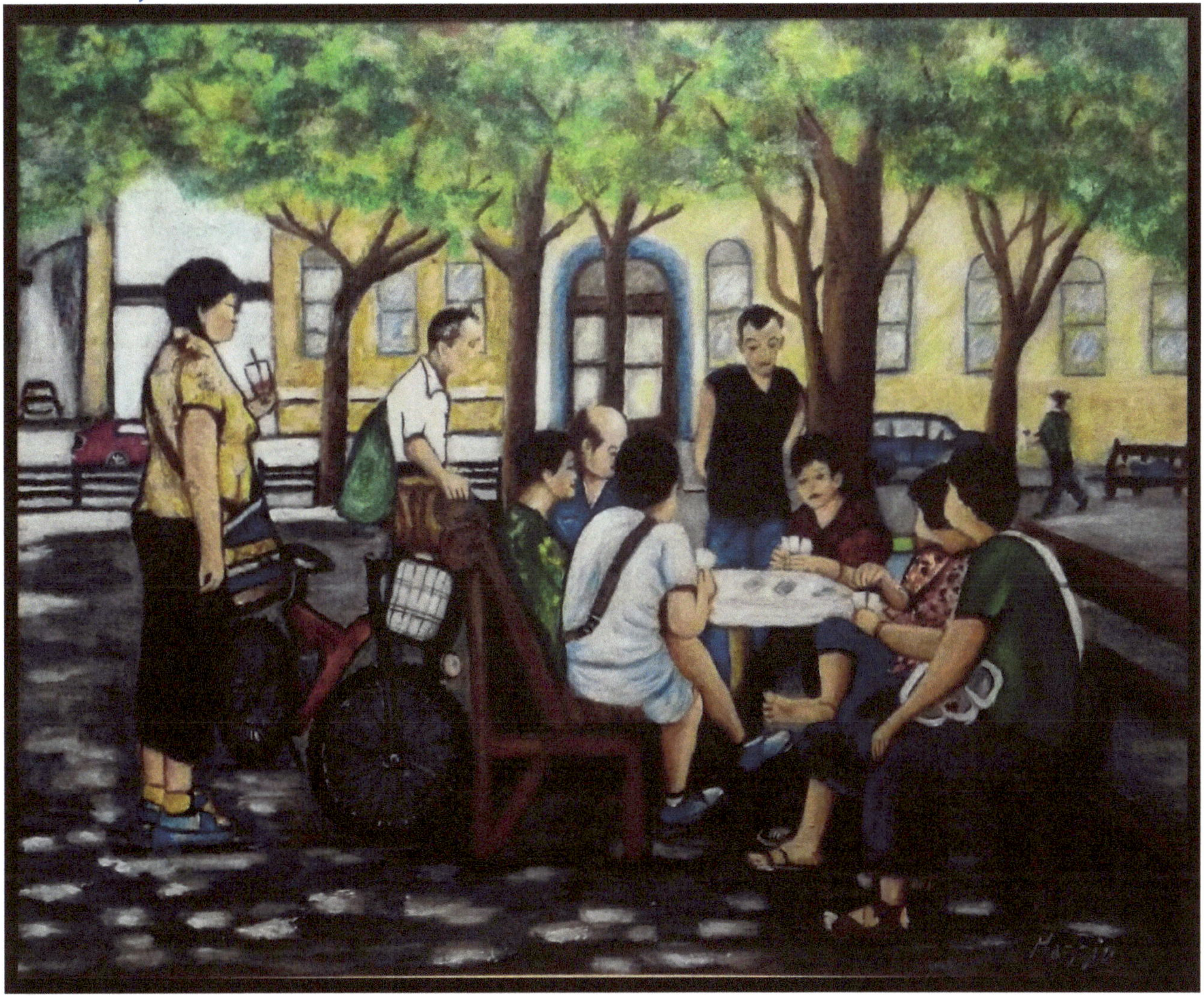

CARDS IN THE PARK by Michael Maggio

Bensonhurst was possibly Brooklyn's best known borough in the 1950s due to its popularity as the fiction home of The Honeymooners. Nowadays it has gone through many years of flux to become a thriving mini-Chinatown of sorts.

This scene is set in a city park along 18th Avenue where local Chinese immigrants congregate daily to walk, practice martial arts, recreate, contemplate and meditate.

Here a group of park regulars play their daily game of *Choi Dai Di* (AKA **Big 2**), keeping their minds sharp, their conversation friendly and their neighborhood safe and inviting. In this 16"x20" oil on canvas **Michael Maggio** cleverly captures the old world ambiance of a population that has moved to a different land but has clearly maintained their cultural and community pride.

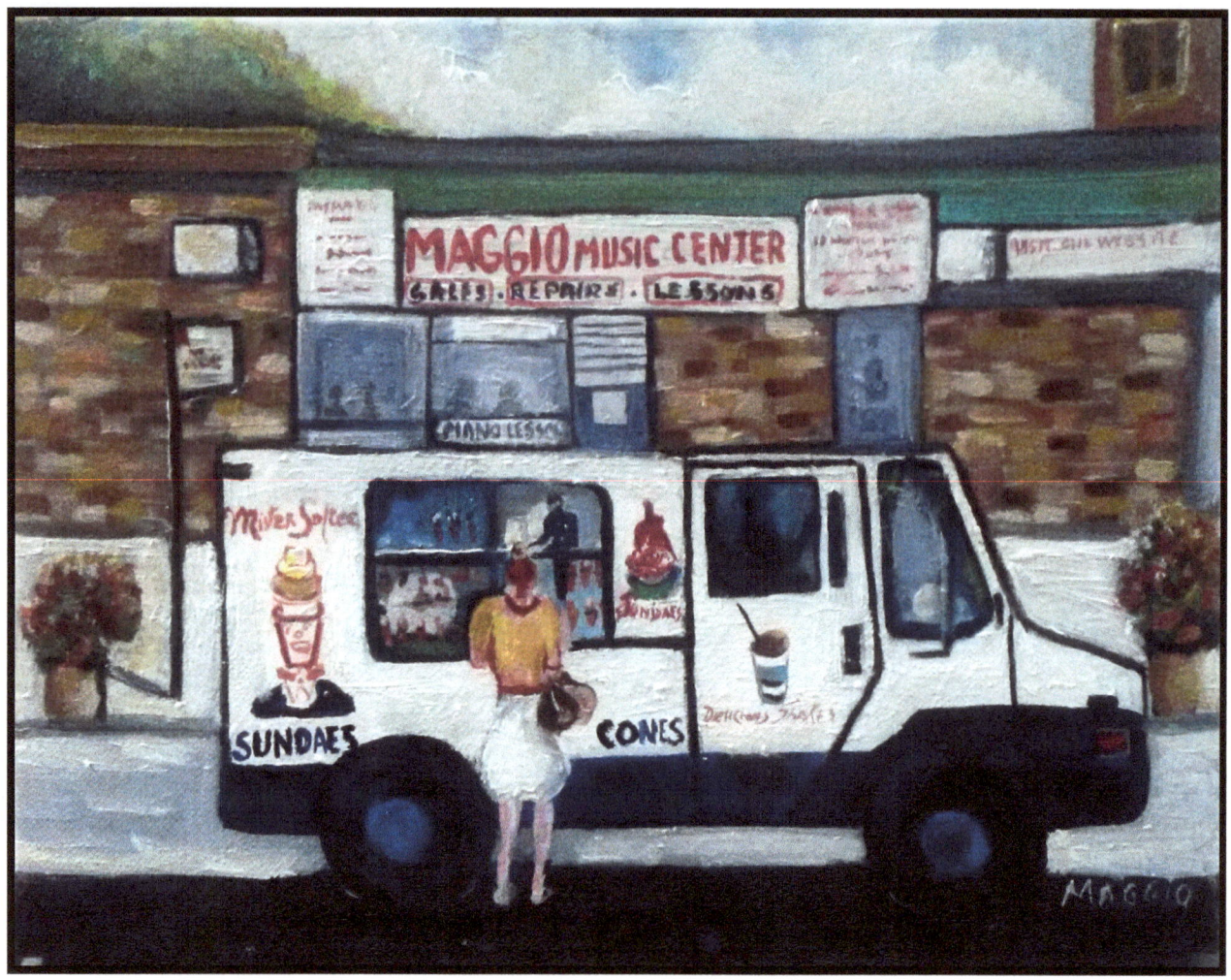

SUMMER STREET MUSIC by Michael Maggio

The summers are scorching along 18th Avenue just a block away from the "El" tracks. That's New York talk for the elevated subway line. The neighborhood is a true mix of ethnicities with Italian, Chinese, Russian and other families calling the area their home.

Maggio Music Center has been a fixture at 8403 18th Avenue since 1937 when it was founded by musician John Maggio. In 1969, Maggio Music was entrusted to our own, Michael Maggio, who took what his father taught him and, with perseverance and hard work, carried on his father's legacy. Michael and his son, Michael, Jr. still own and manage the business.

Michael Maggio has imagined a warm summer's day when the center may be filled with budding musicians honing their talents while pedestrians are lured to the siren call of an omnipresent Mister Softees, whose musical bells promise a cold delicious treat. The oil on canvas tableau is a cool 9"x12".

For more information see: ***www.maggiomusicschool.com***

Brooklyn DYKER HEIGHTS

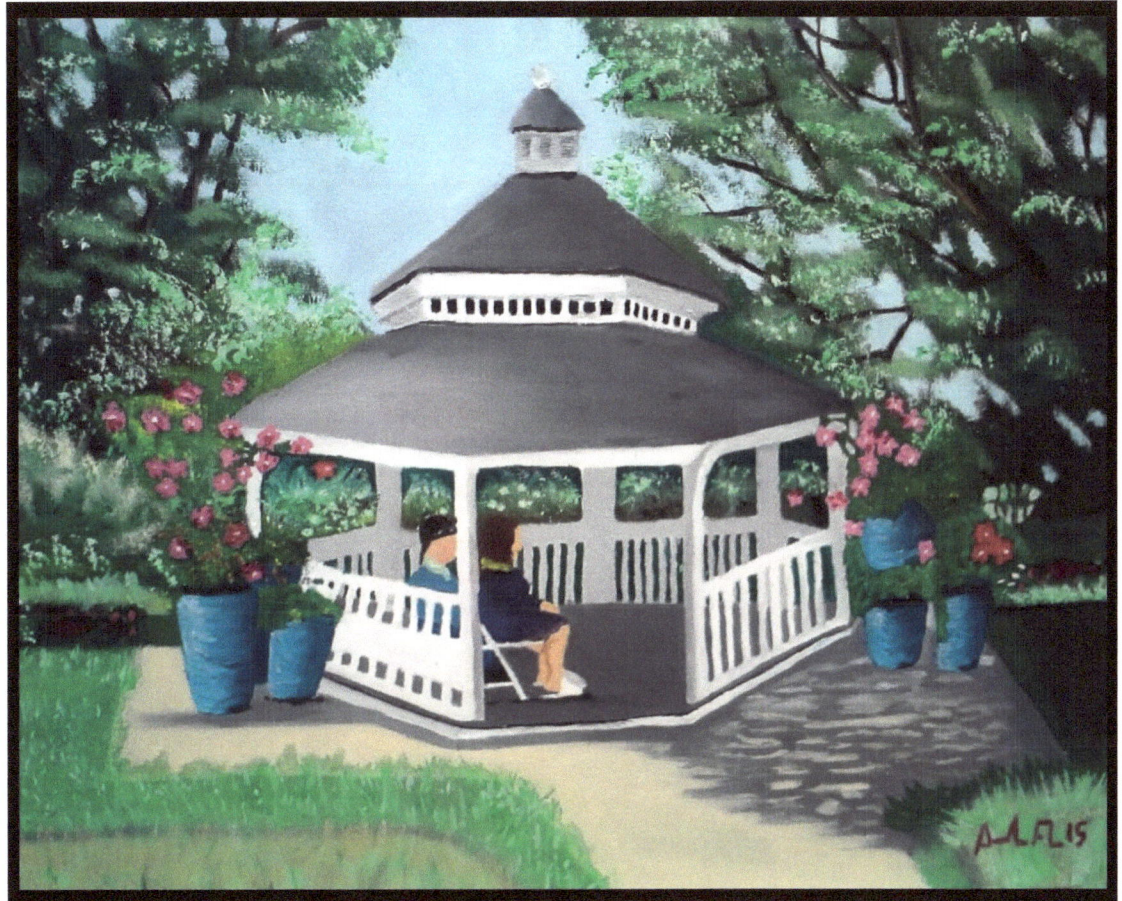

THE DYKER GAZEBO by Amber Furey-Lessen

The **Dyker Beach Golf Course** is a championship grade par 72 course that sits just below the Verrazano Bridge and, not coincidentally, directly across the street from **Michael's Private Painting Instructions**.   One of the jewels of the course's club and catering service is the picturesque **gazebo** that is often the centerpiece of many weddings and ceremonies.

The course itself was originally designed by Tom Bendelow in 1897, then redesigned by Jon Van Kleek in 1935. The gazebo has been enchanting visitors for decades.

Amber Furey-Lessen painted the gazebo in 2015 in its everyday, non-business setting as a quiet sitting place for folks to meet, relax, read or mediate. The 18-year old's 16"x20" oil on canvas colorfully reminds us that, even in the hustle and bustle of modern city life, Brooklyn still retains its fair share of quiet nooks and crannies that can evoke the peaceful demeanor of days gone by.

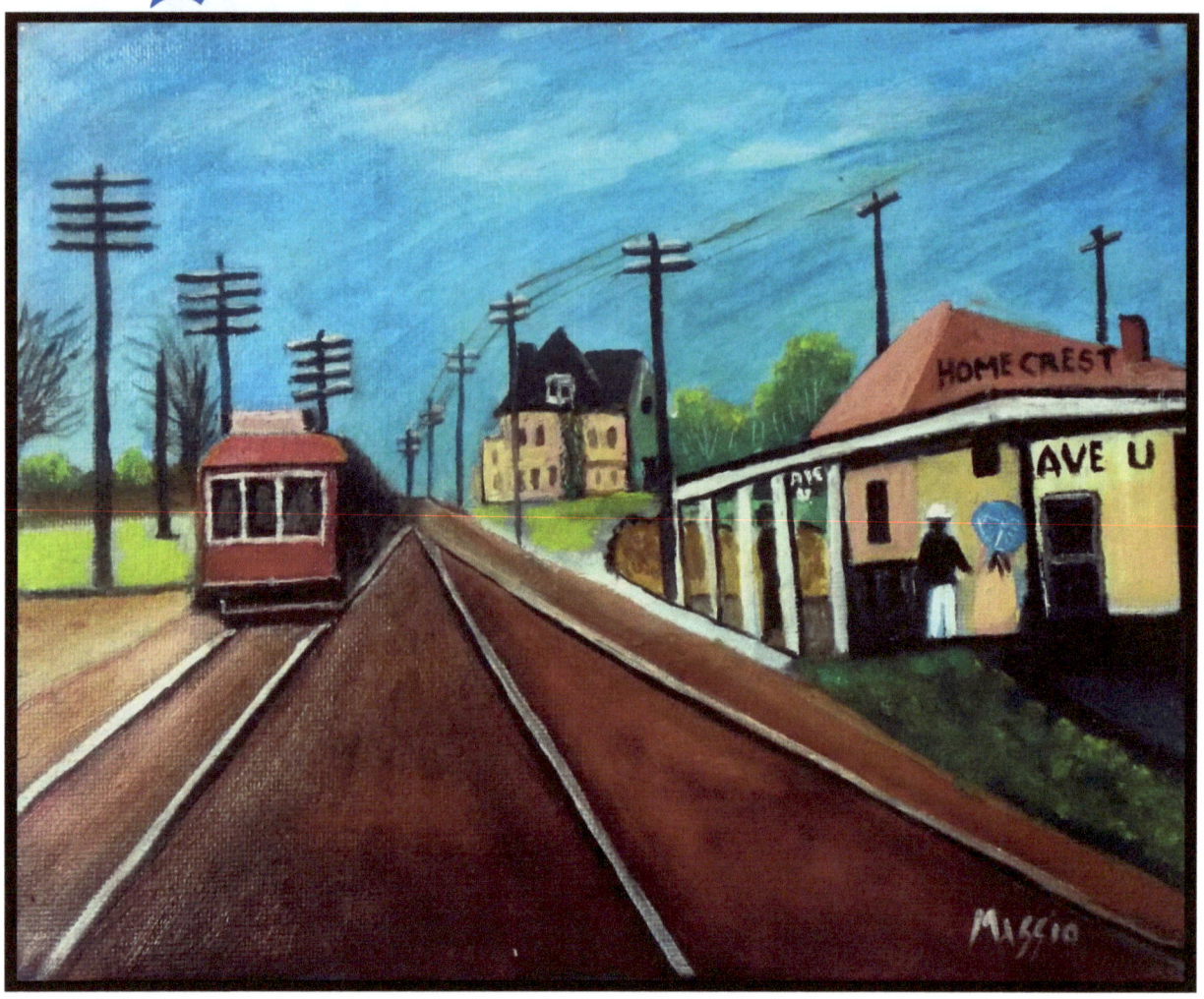

AVENUE U TROLLEY by Michael Maggio

It's fairly well known that turn-of-the-century Brooklyn's residents were highly skilled at dodging the electric horsecars of their extensive trolley system.   This led to the borough's citizens being dubbed "Brooklyn Dodgers".

By the early 1900s Brooklyn had become one of the most modernized locales in the entire country with trolley lines criss-crossing their way throughout the entirety of Brooklyn town, even in the quieter, relatively rural sections of Gravesend.

Michael Maggio's pictureque presentation of the vintage Coney Island line, depicting the station at Avenue U and Homecrest Avenue, circa 1901 is a beautiful 9"x12" oil on canvas recalling a simpler and quainter era in the borough's proud history.

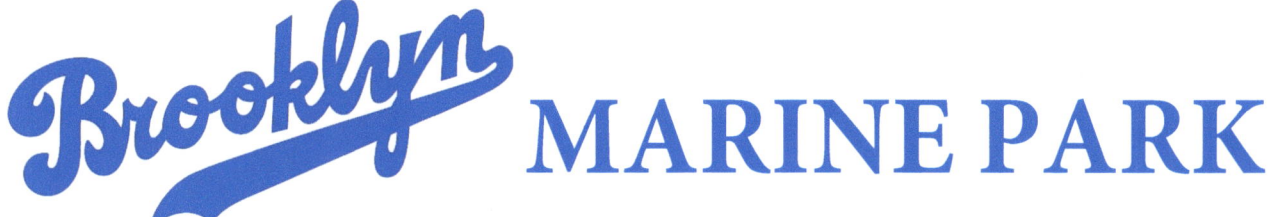

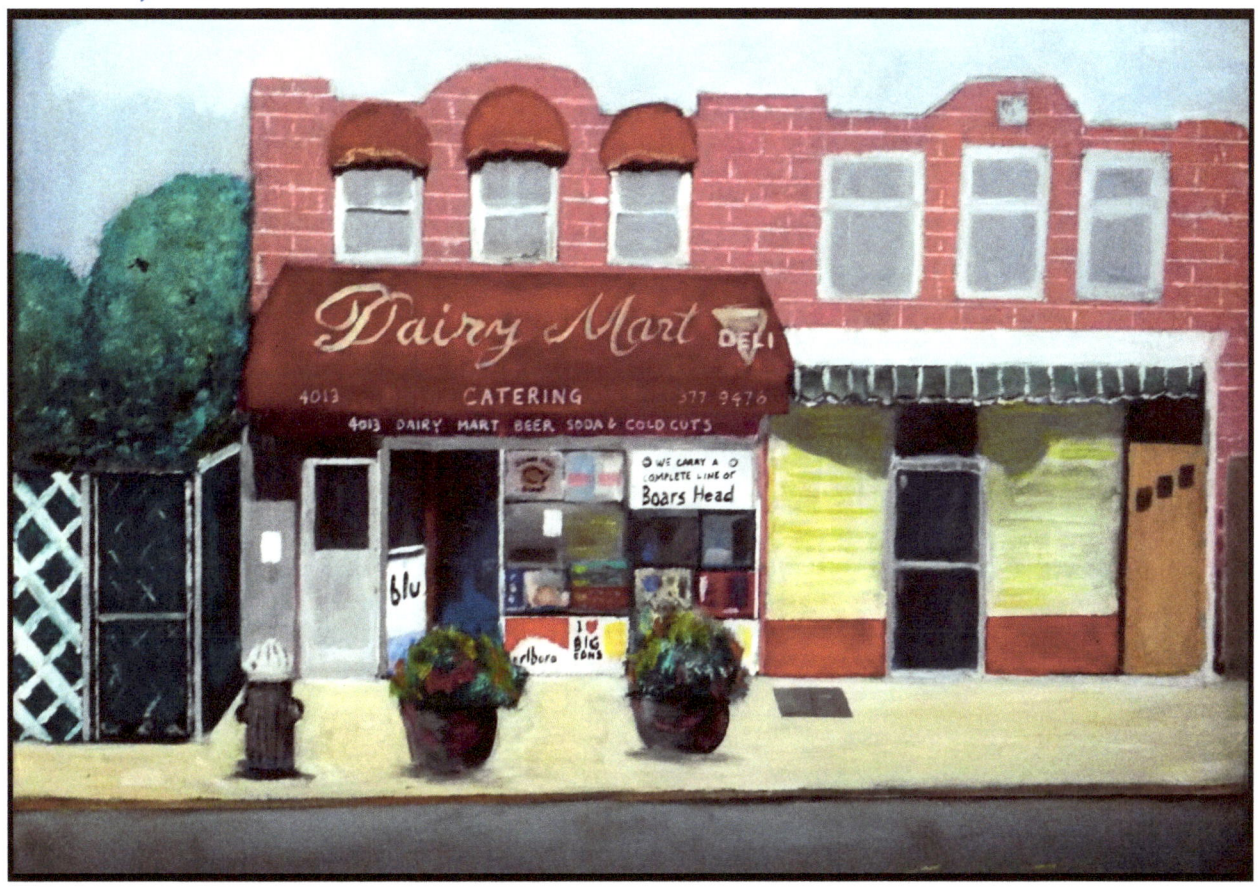

MY FAVORITE DELI by Katie Collins

There are over 3000 delicatessens in Brooklyn and no neighborhood is complete without its own. Everybody's favorite deli is always the one just down the street or around the corner. The borough is dotted with Jewish delis, Russian delis, Korean delis, Polish delis, Irish delis, German delis, and on and on.

Nestled amongst the quiet homes on Avenue T in Marine Park is **Dairy Mart** – best known to neighborhood residents as *Mrs. Lee's Deli*. Featuring typical deli fare (sandwiches, heroes, coffee, cold cuts, salads, soups, mini-grocery and just about anything else you'd need to get through a typical Brooklyn day), Juliana and Joe Lee have been greeting customers with smiles and deli-delicious food at inviting prices for 19 years now.

Katie Collins painted her favorite deli when she was 11 years old using oil on canvas. The original 16"x20" painting is now proudly hanging in the deli's entrance.

Brooklyn MARINE PARK

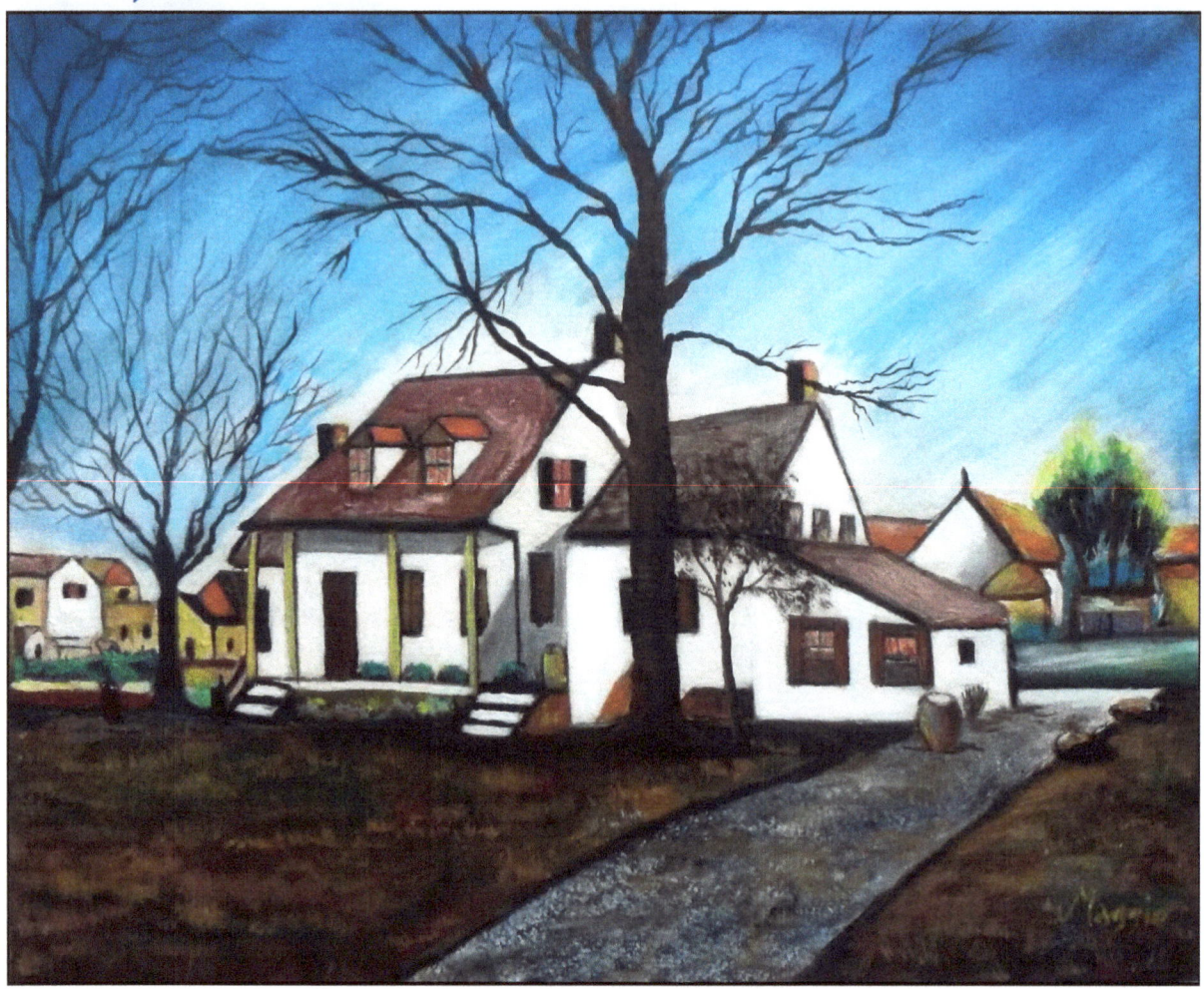

THE LOTT HOUSE by Michael Maggio

Nestled in the heart of Marine Park is the historic farm home best known as the **Hendrick I. Lott House**. Flanked on all sides by relatively modern frame homes constructed in the mid-1900s, The Lott House was constructed by Hendrick Lott in 1800 on land that was part of his grandfather Johannes Lott's original homestead from 1720. The home is one of the oldest Dutch Colonial farmhouses in Brooklyn and has been declared an official landmark by the National Register of Historic Places. It stands proudly at 1940 East 36th Street.

Michael Maggio painted this grand representation of the current Lott House as a 16" by 20" oil on canvas in March 2016. To this day the house basically remains structurally unchanged from its original construction.

More information at *nycgovparks.org/parks/hendrick-i-lott-house/history*

Brooklyn JAMAICA BAY SALT MARSH

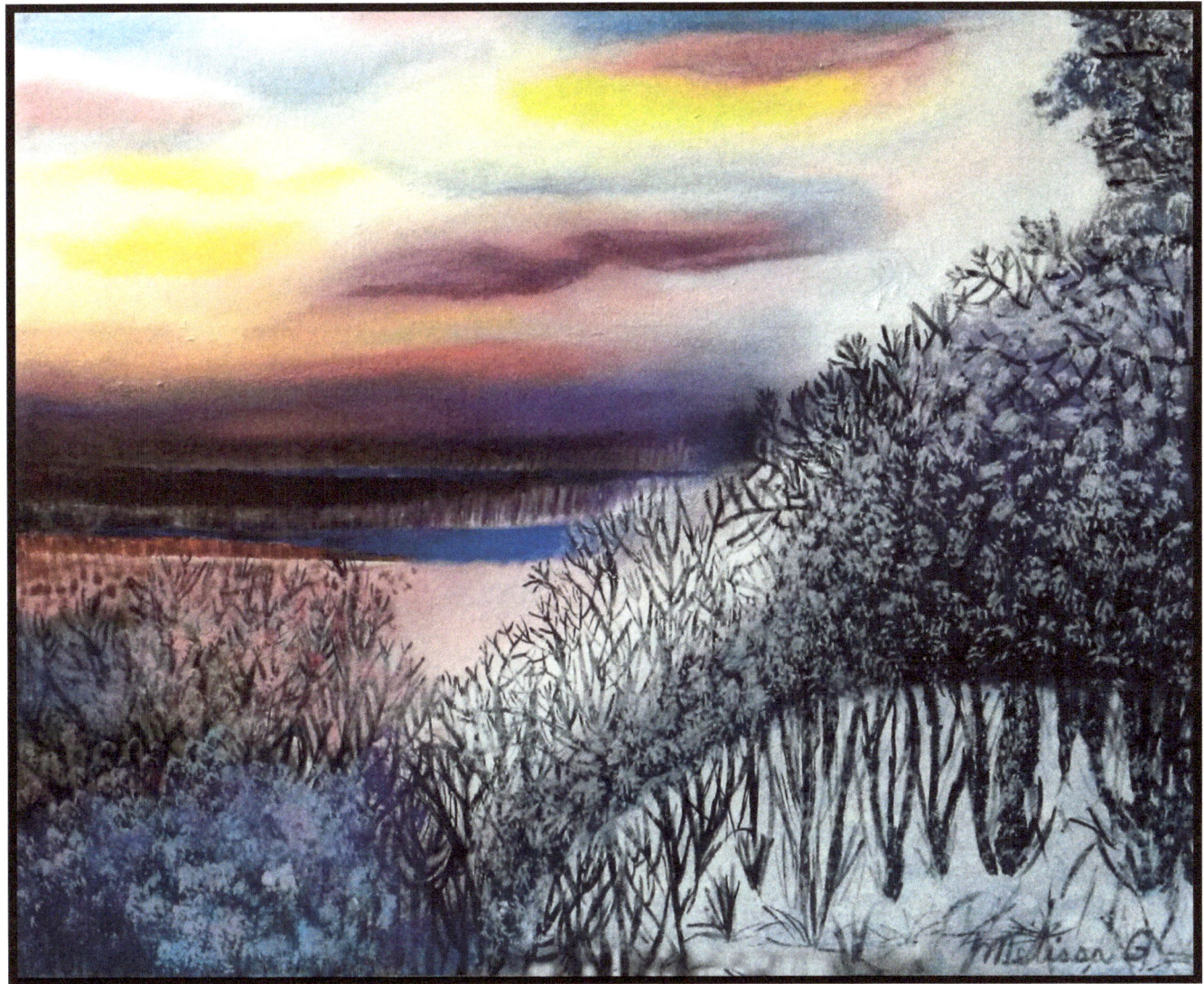

SALT MARSH IN WINTER by Melissa Gonzalez

The **Salt Marsh Nature Center** might be Brooklyn's greatest secret. Flora and fauna thrive literally just yards away from busy avenues and parkways. One can walk or sit and take in the amazing wonders of running rabbits, soaring osprey, dancing butterflys, and so much more. 530 acres of grassland and salt marsh are home to many species you probably didn't even know existed in Brooklyn and it's all there at the southern tip of Marine Park in an area once known as the swamps.

Dedicated animal activist **Melissa Gonzales** froze this wintry marsh scene in oil on a 16"x20" canvas. In her time away from her work in the medical field, Melissa cherishes spending as much time as possible with her daughter and playing with her chihuahua, Diesel, who is seen at right in one of Michael Maggio's hand painted tambourines.

21

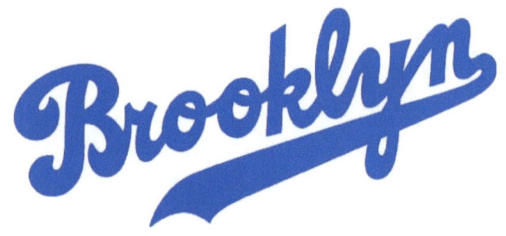

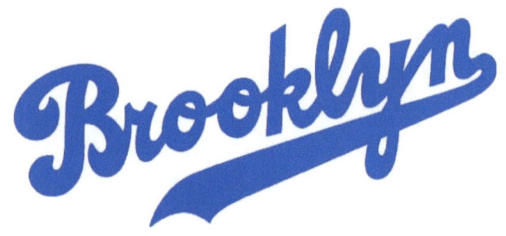

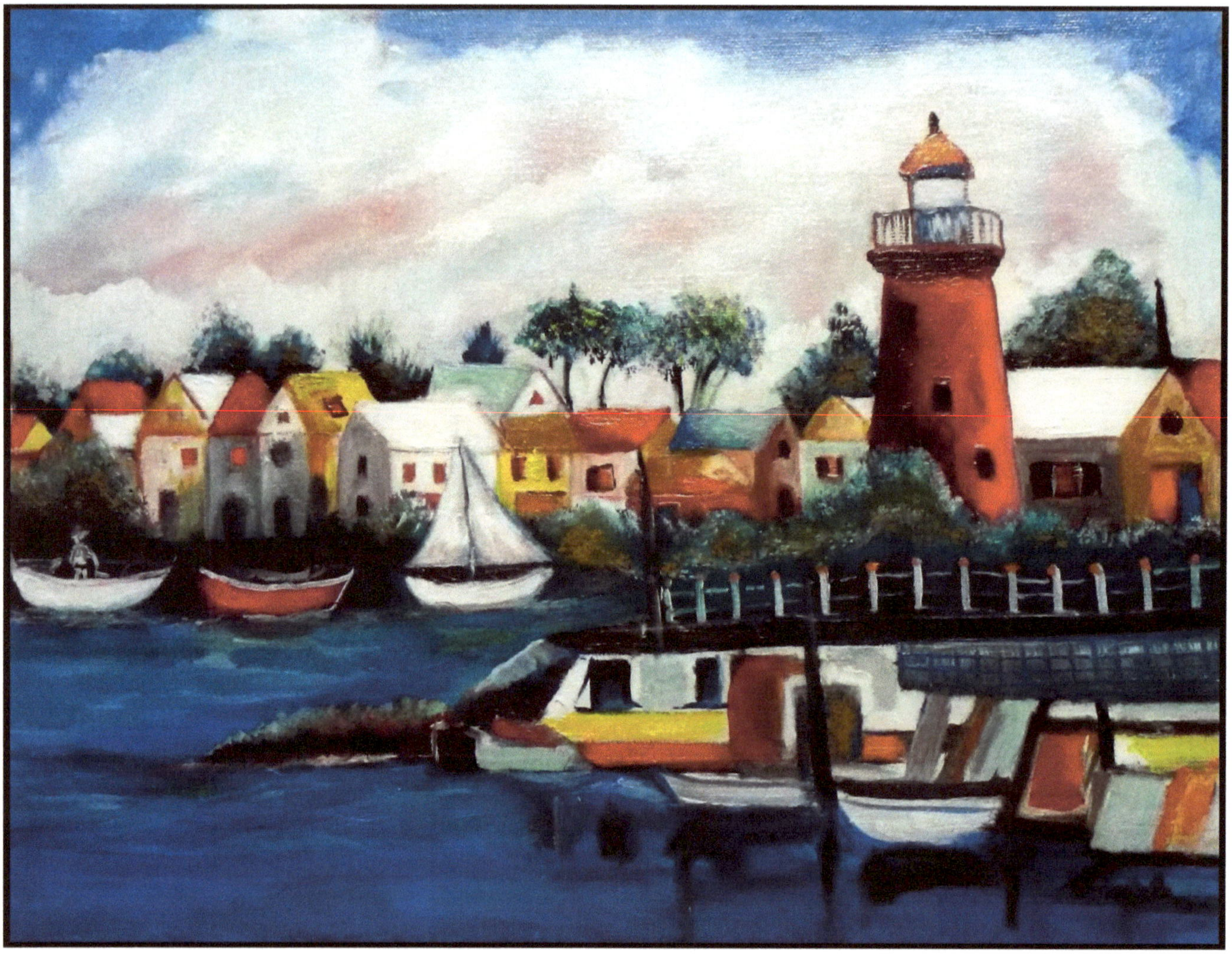

THE SHEEPSHEAD LIGHTHOUSE by Michael Maggio

Jordan's Lobster Dock began serving New York in 1938 on Bleeker Street in Manhattan. Serving fresh Maine- and Canadian-imported lobsters to hungry New Yorkers found the business booming and growing, eventually to Brooklyn and Island Park. The popular Sheepshead Bay location on Harkness Avenue off of Knapp Street features a quaint mock lighthouse that oversees the ships and boats of both commercial and private fishermen who live and work on the bay and attracts seafood lovers from miles around.

Michael Maggio 's rustic rendition of the lighthouse shows off Brooklyn's lifelong love affair with the inlets off of Jamaica Bay. The colorful eye-opening image is 12"x16" oil on canvas.

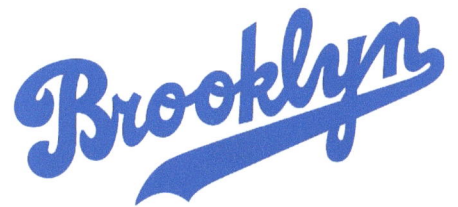

FLATBUSH CELEBRITY

One of Brooklyn's most cherished celebrities is Flatbush's own songstress and actress, the Funny Girl herself, **Barbra Streisand**.

Barbra was born and bred in Flatbush, Brooklyn in April of 1942. She was one of the famous celebrity students at Erasmus High School on Flatbush Avenue.

She has sold over 145-million records worldwide in her career and she garnered numerous Grammy Awards and Academy Awards.

An odd fact: Barbra never publicly performed in her native Brooklyn until the inaugurals of the Barclay Center in 2012.

Michael Maggio preserved prime time Barbra with an airbrush in this large form masterpiece.

Michael has excelled in capturing celebrity likenesses not only in oil but with pastels and using an airbrush.

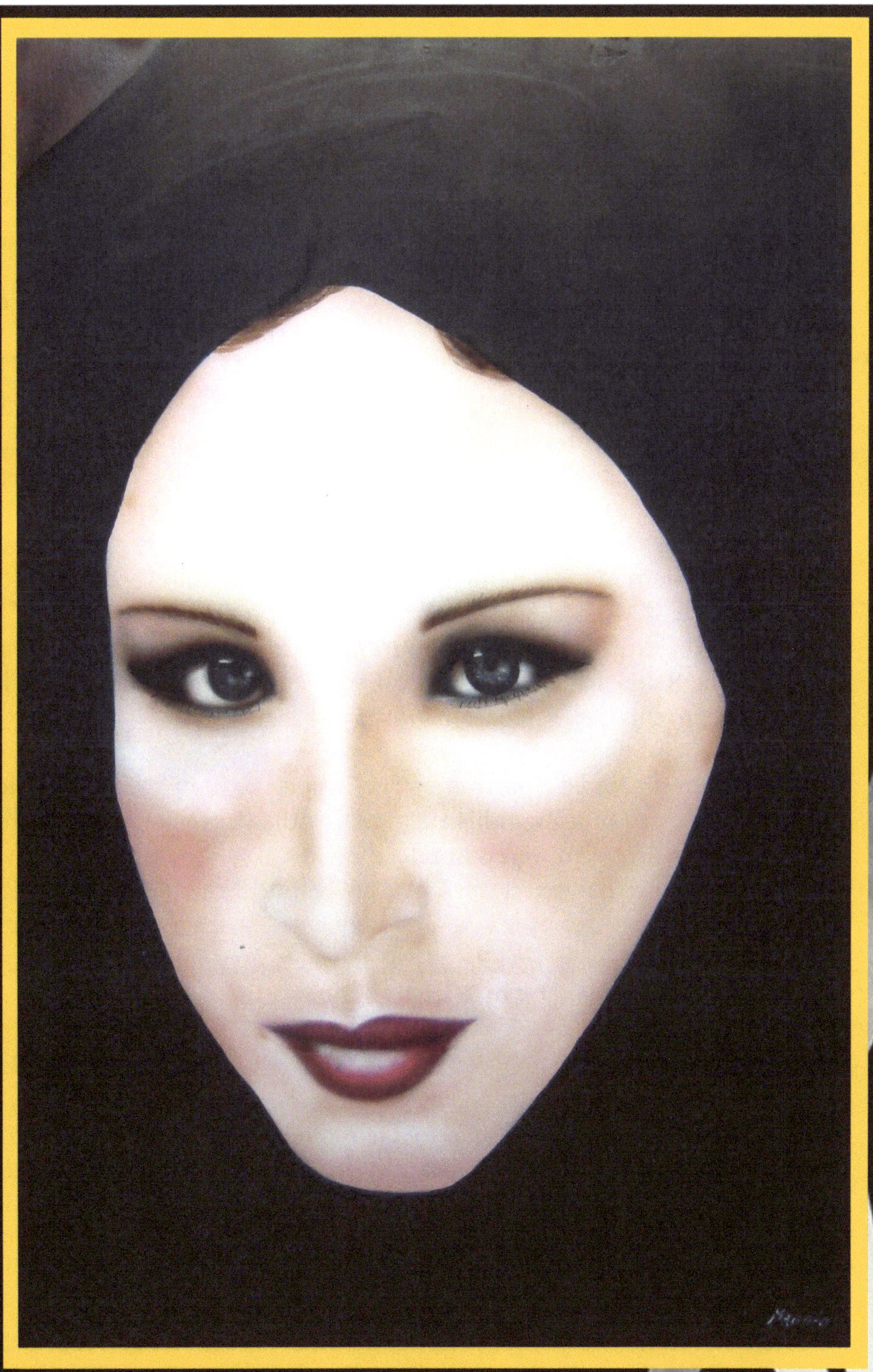

BARBRA STREISAND by MICHAEL MAGGIO

Students at Maggio Painting Instructions have the option of learning any of these methods from Michael.

Michael is no stranger to fame and the famous and you can see more of his celebrity images on page 26.

23

Brushes with Fame

Artists often reflect the culture of a period and sometimes they are the best recorders of a given period.

As a transplanted Brooklynite, we've just seen that Michael Maggio was deeply impressed by one of Brooklyn's own, **Barbra Streisand**.

In his travels around the world – Brooklyn and beyond – Michael has encountered the rich and famous and has tasted a little of bit of celebrity himself.

For example, in the early 1990's while he was still doing the heavy lifting at his family's **Maggio's Music Center** on 18th Avenue, he had occasion to be delivering a key board to a customer in the Crown Heights neighborhood of Brooklyn. As he prepared, Michael noticed a large group of Hasidic Jews walking in his direction. Going on with his business of moving the keyboard, Michael was soon in the midst of this movable congregation and was face-to-face with **Menachem Mendel Schneerson**, known to his followers as The Rebbe or The Messiah. The Rebbe and Michael embraced and the great man asked Michael if he happened to be Jewish. "*No*," Michael replied, "*I'm Italian*." After an exchange of laughs and some kind words, The Rebbe handed Michael a memorial card and asked him to keep it with him at all times and, to this day, Michael has done just that.

Later, Michael painted a portrait of The Rebbe and hung it in his studio. A local radio station even interviewed him about his encounter with Schneerson and his venerable painting. Jews from all over Brooklyn were soon flocking to the studio to meet with Michael and to kiss his hand – the hand that was clasped by The Rebbe, the hand that painting his portrait.

In 2000, Michael's oil portrait of **Tony Bennett** so caught the long-time entertainer's eye that he insisted upon signing it to Michael. Today it is one of Michael's most cherished paintings.

About four years ago, Michael with in an uptown funk club to see and listen to jazz great **Ahmed Jamal** who had just recently been inducted into the *American Jazz Hall of Fame* and was named a *Living Jazz Legend by the Kennedy Center for the Performing Arts*. Michael slipped into Jamal's dressing room and had a quiet fulfilling conversation with the performer. Michael just wanted to pick the brain of a living genius and to discuss his craft, talent and impressions. After their talk, Michael painted a portrait of Jamal and, to this day, the likeness of the legend still hangs proudly in Michael's home.

Here we present a very small selection of some of Michael's eclectic collection of famous faces and modern day celebrities, both the rich and the famous.

Michael Maggio's Famous Faces

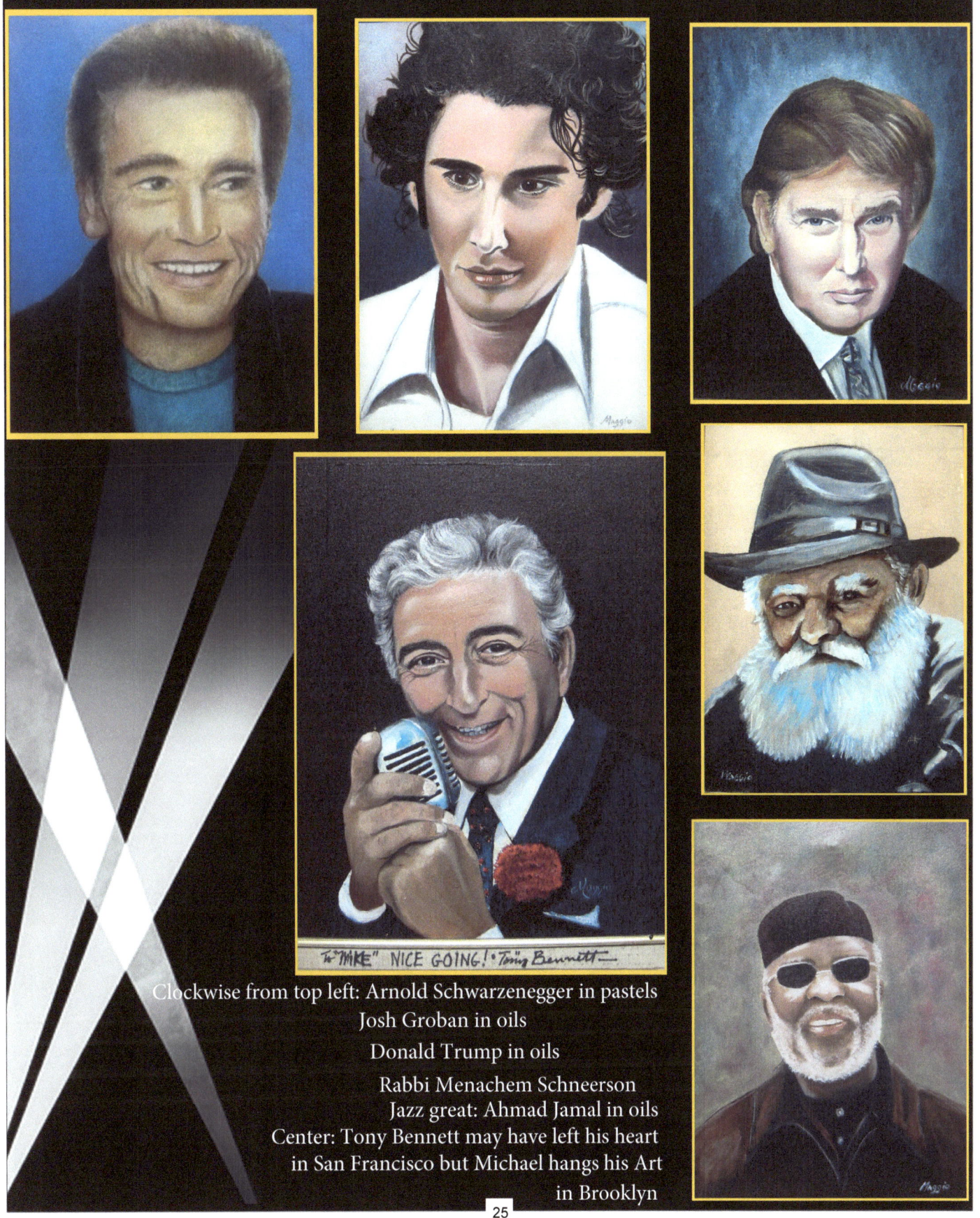

Clockwise from top left: Arnold Schwarzenegger in pastels
Josh Groban in oils
Donald Trump in oils
Rabbi Menachem Schneerson
Jazz great: Ahmad Jamal in oils
Center: Tony Bennett may have left his heart
in San Francisco but Michael hangs his Art
in Brooklyn

THE ART AND ARTISTS
OF
MICHAEL'S PAINTING INSTRUCTIONS

Parrot Place is the quaintly name street that's basically a short offshoot of 7th Avenue in Bay Ridge. Sitting unassumingly at 6 Parrot Place is a tiny art studio that bustles with the strokes and dabbings of budding Picassos, Rembrandts and Van Goghs five days per week.

Aspiring artists first learn the basics of the craft from Michael Maggio and then they are free to explore their imaginations, choosing their own subjects and sharpening their skills at their own speed.

There is never any pressure on Michael's students to advance at any given pace and no one with a set of brushes and a supply of paint is ever discouraged or turned away.

Michael teaches all the basic painting styles and in just about every medium: oils, acrylic, water color, air brushing, and pastels. Special attention is given whenever students request help in specific areas of improvement, such as sketching or blending colors and such.

Everybody's welcome at Michaels and, now, we'd like to introduce you to some of the regular students and their proud creations.

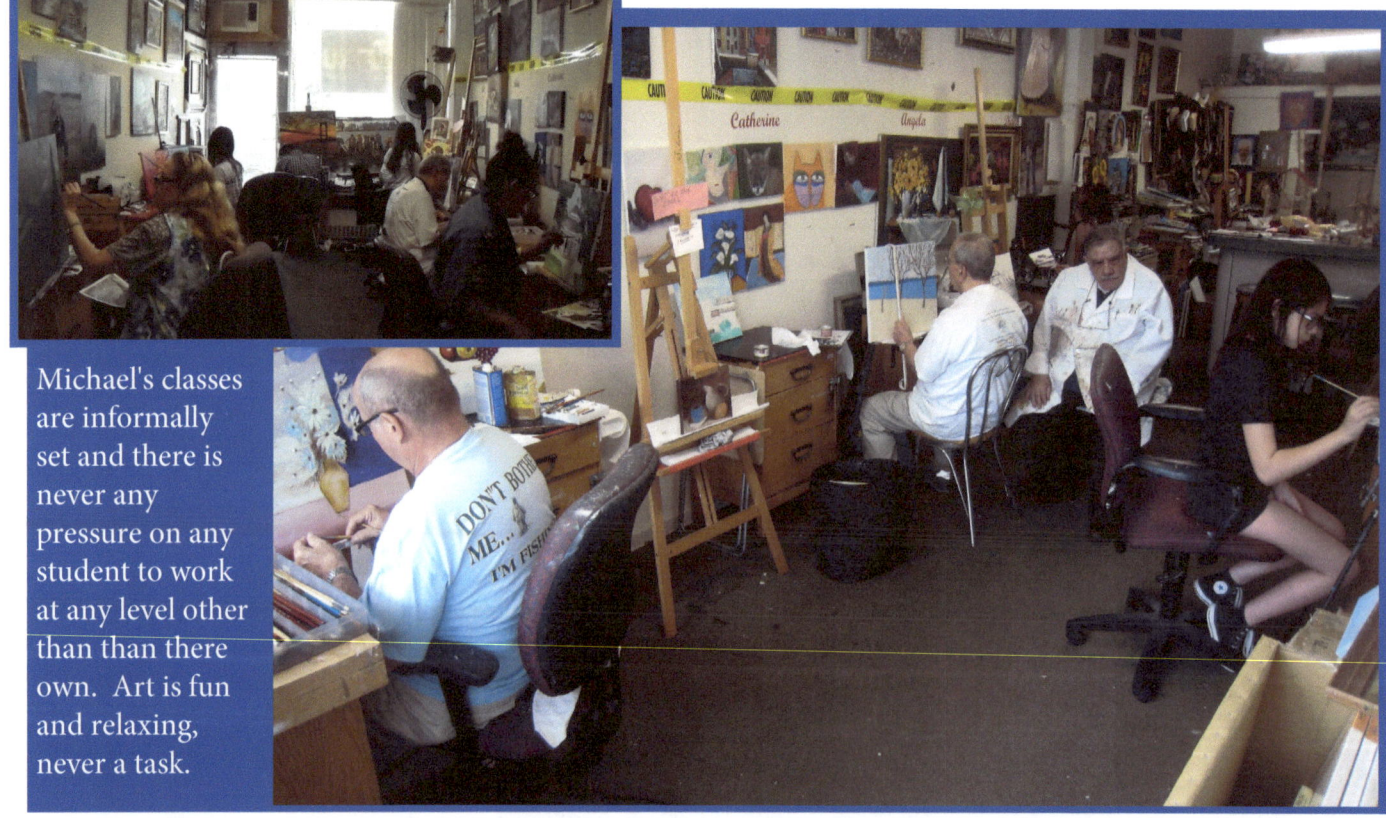

Michael's classes are informally set and there is never any pressure on any student to work at any level other than than there own. Art is fun and relaxing, never a task.

The Artists of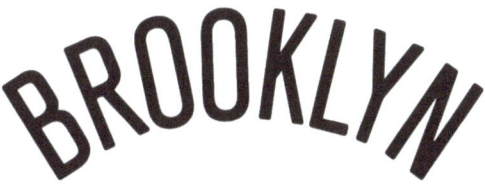

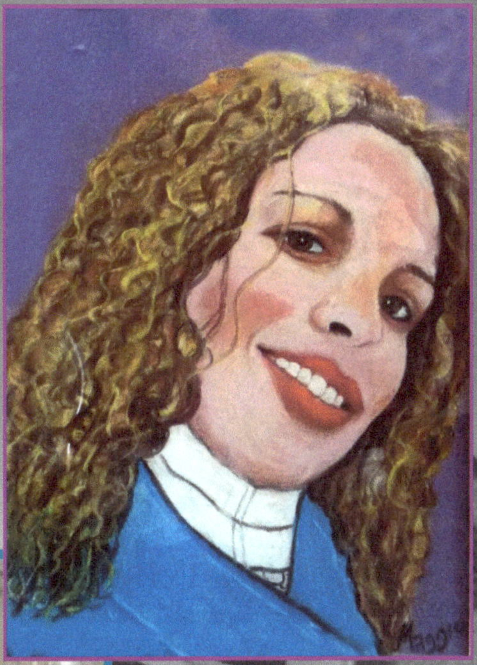

Michael Maggio enshrined his student **Melissa Gonzalez** in pastels

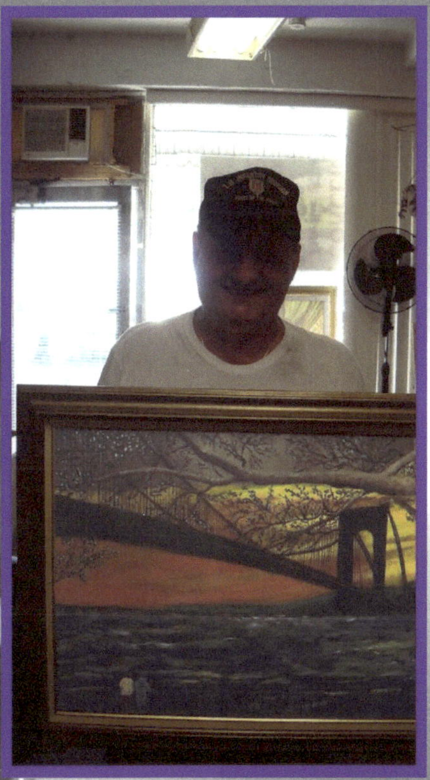

Vinny Fina proudly displays his oil on canvas of the **Verrazano Bridge**

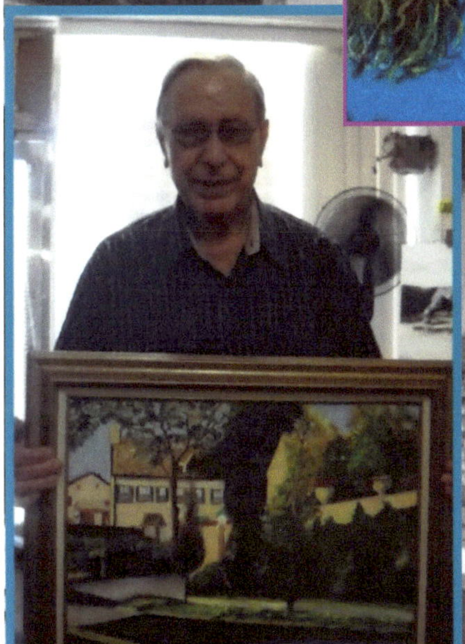

Retired **Dr. Michael Gabriel** put his own Bay Ridge home on canvas

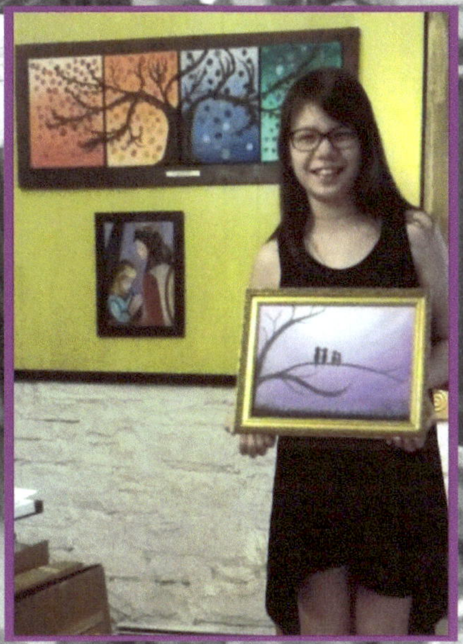

Katie Collins poses with three of her favorite oil paintings

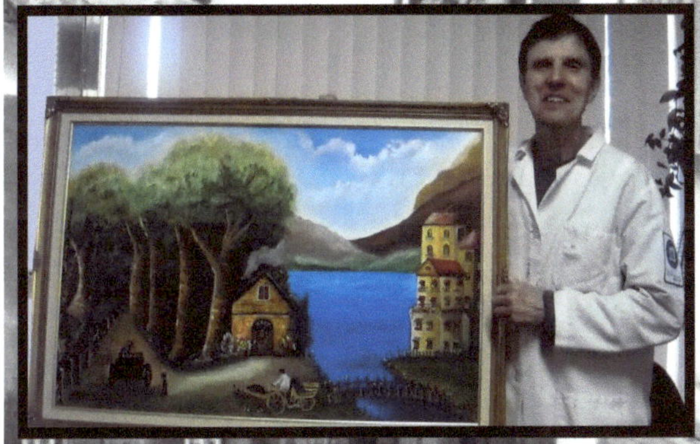

Giovanni Randazzo imagined this spectacular Italian pastoral.

The Artists of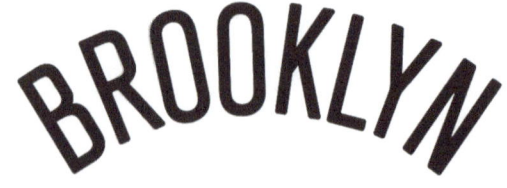

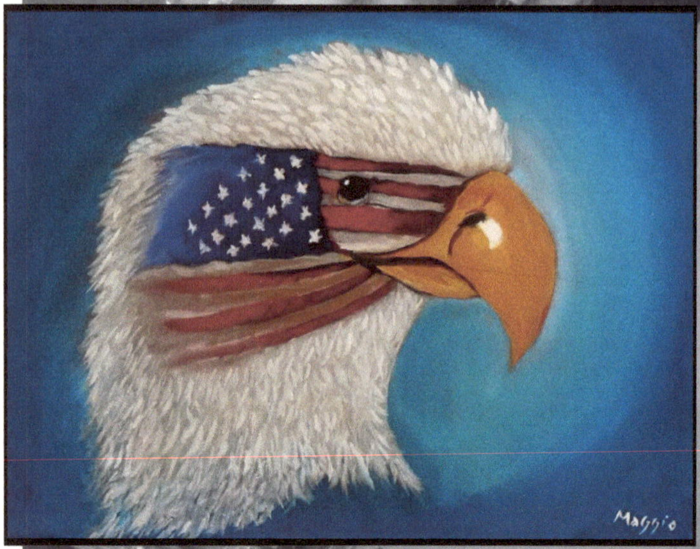

"American Resolve"
by Michael Maggio

Painted in aftermath
of September 11, 2001
12"x16" oil on canvas

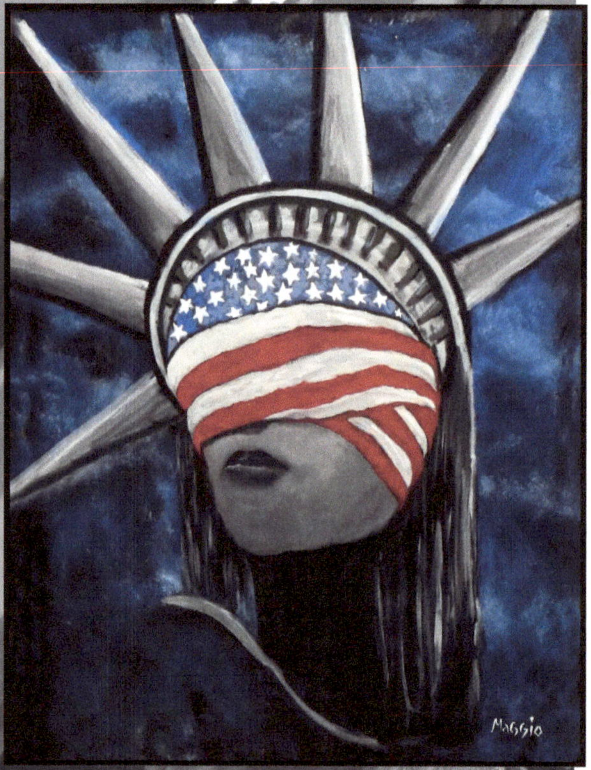

"Liberty Looks Away"
by Michael Maggio

Painted in aftermath of September 11, 2001
16"x20" oil on canvas

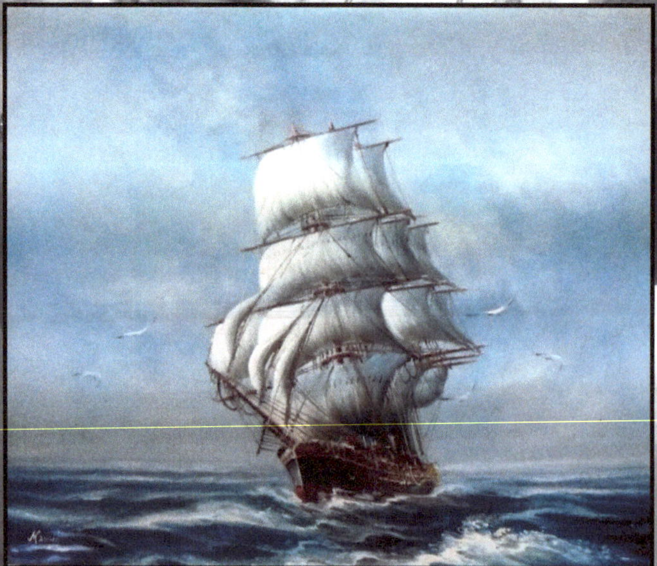

**"Over the
Bounding Main"**

by Michael Maggio

Painted in 1990
16"x20" oil on canvas

The Artists of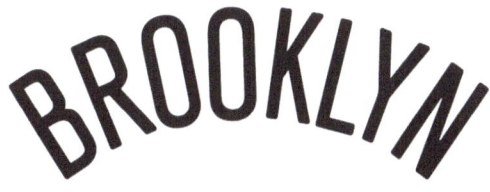

Amber Furey-Lessen and the Dyker Gazebo

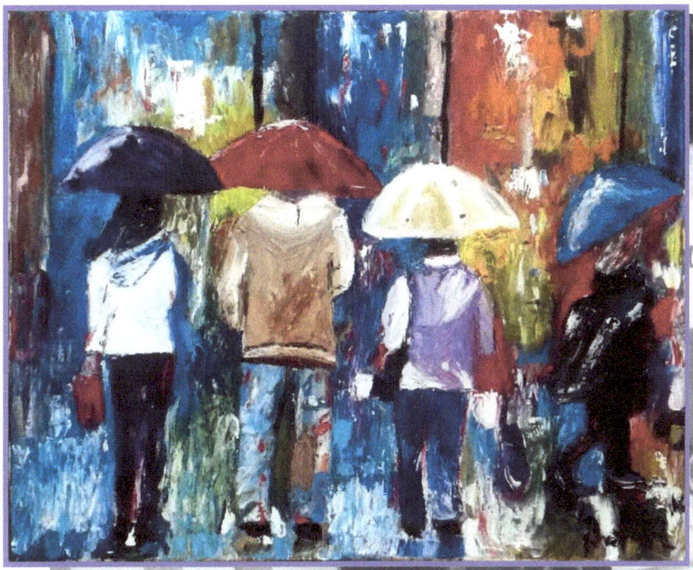

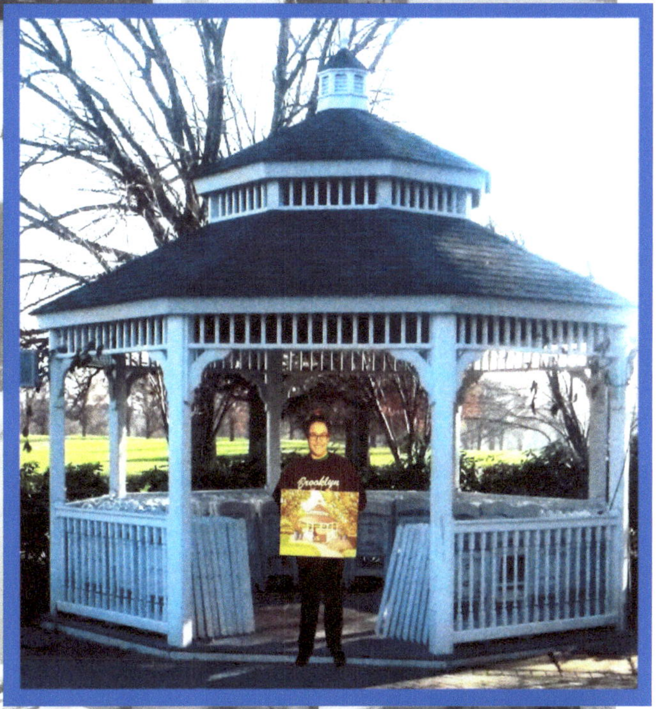

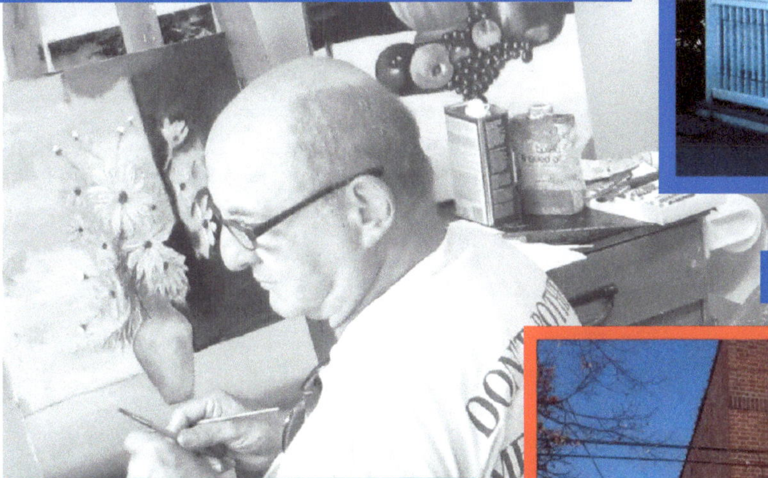

Amber Furey-Lessen's striking exercise in knife and oils.

Katie Collins in front of Dairy Mart

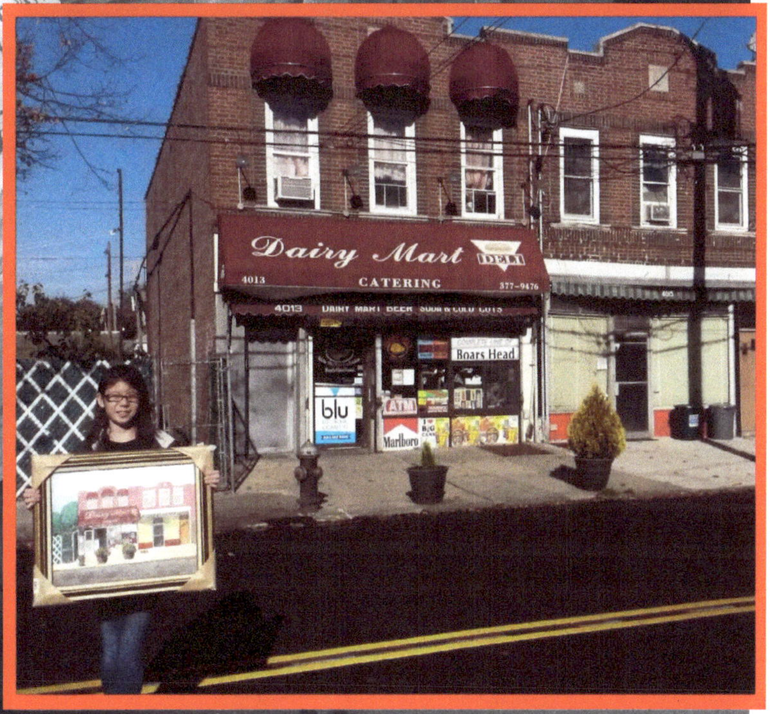

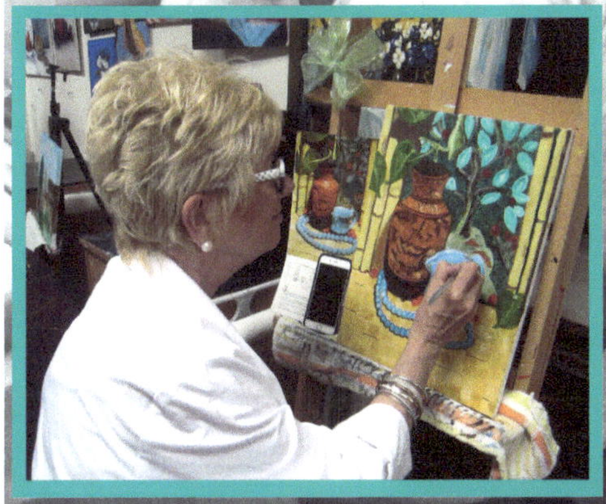

Diana Howe works on her very first still life

The Artists of BROOKLYN

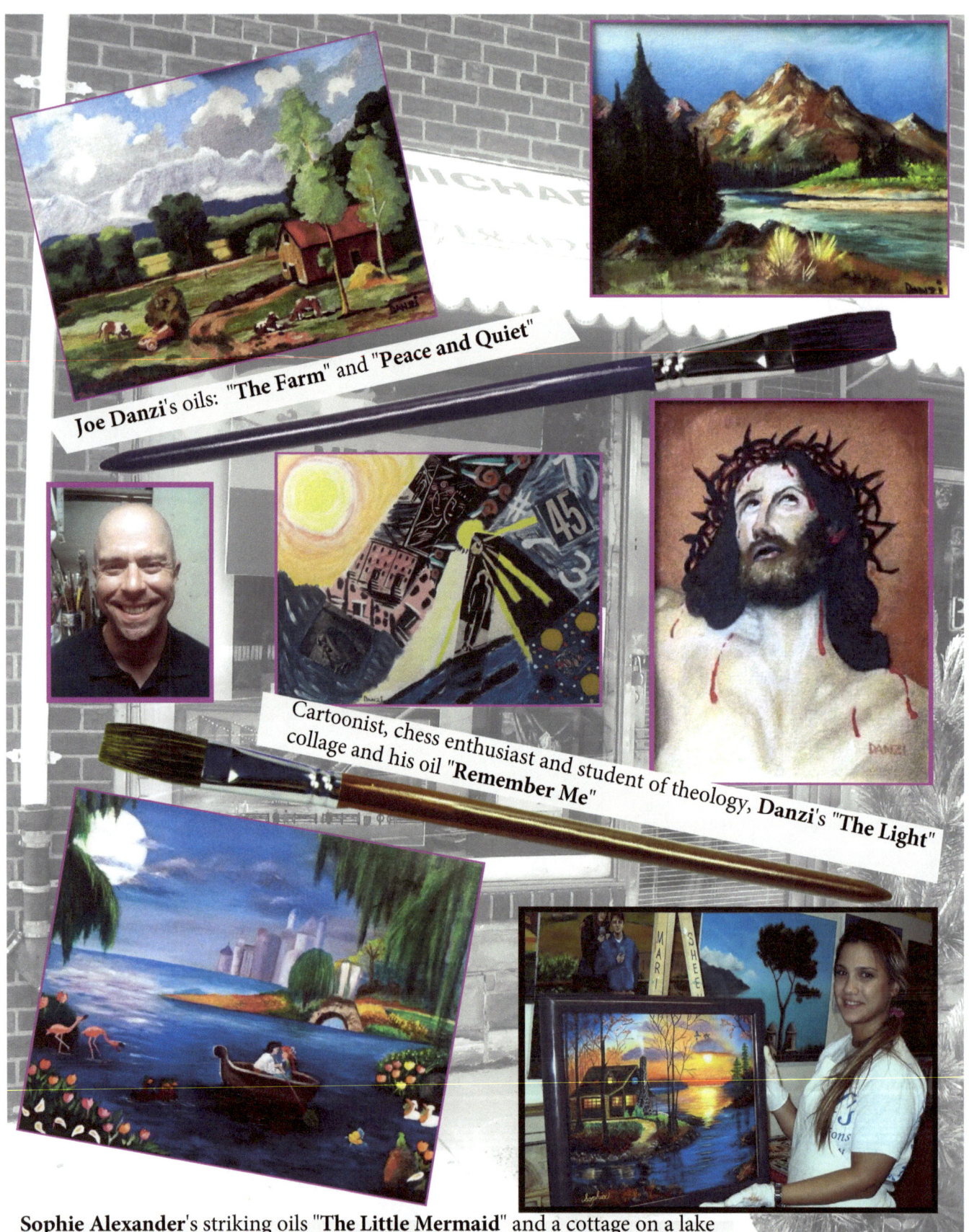

Joe Danzi's oils: "**The Farm**" and "**Peace and Quiet**"

Cartoonist, chess enthusiast and student of theology, Danzi's "**The Light**" collage and his oil "**Remember Me**"

Sophie Alexander's striking oils "**The Little Mermaid**" and a cottage on a lake

The Artists of BROOKLYN

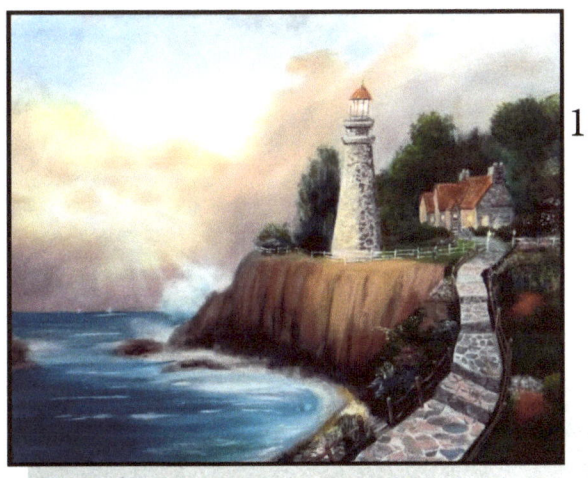

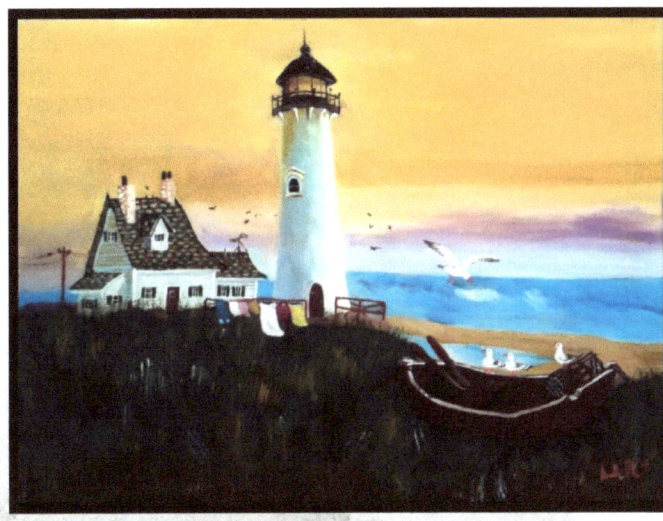

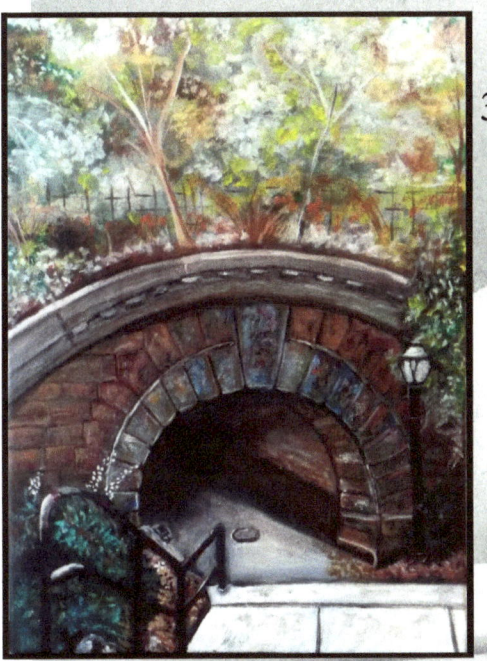

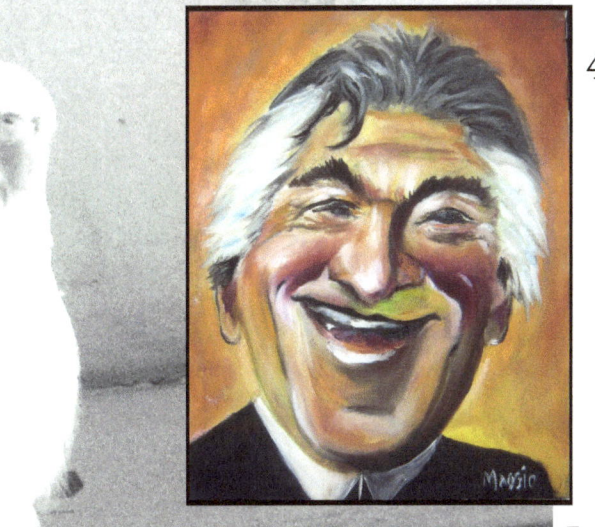

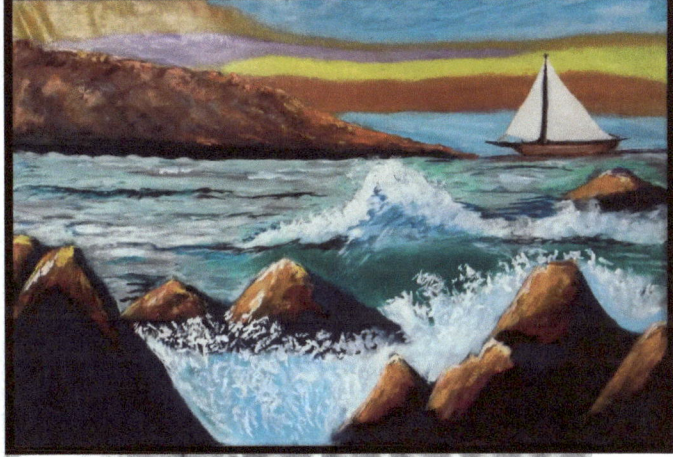

1 - **John Kemp**'s Lighthouse
2 - **Amber Furey-Lessen**'s
     Lighthouse
3 - **Michael Maggio**'s Central Park
4 - **Michael Maggio**'s caricature of
     Robert De Niro
5 - **Vinny Fina**'s Scene from a
     Shoreline

Michael Maggio's
IMPRESSIONS of 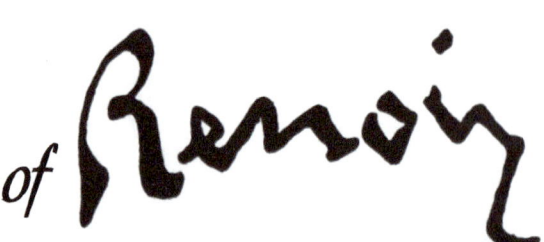 Renoir

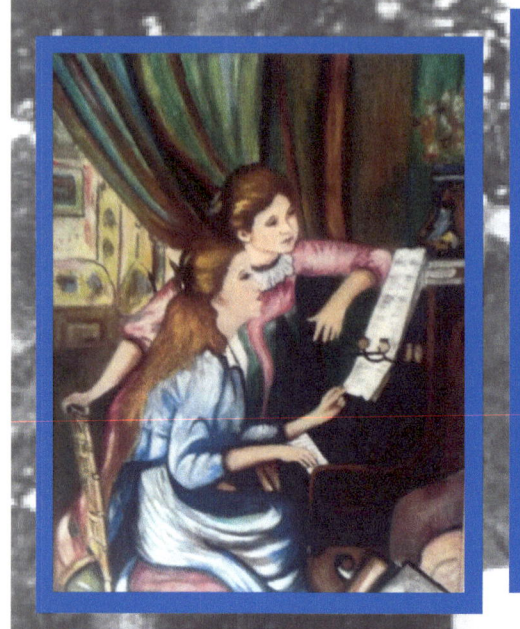

"Girls at the Piano"

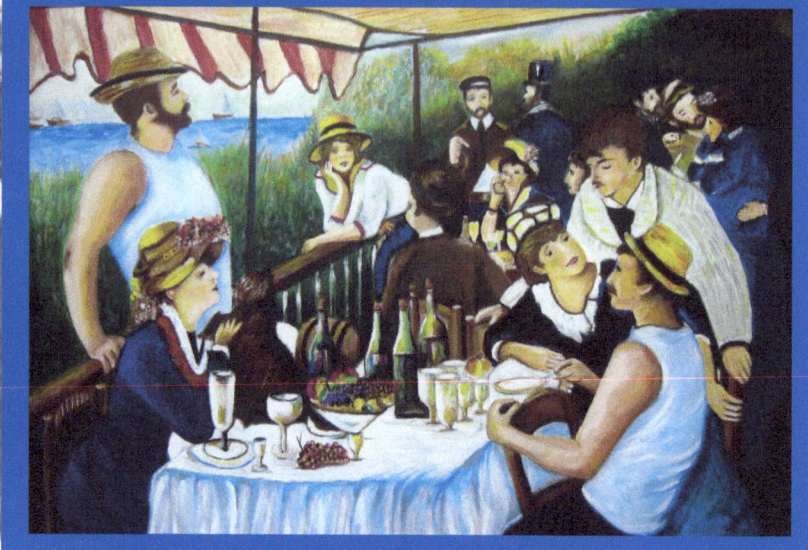

"The Boating Party Lunch"

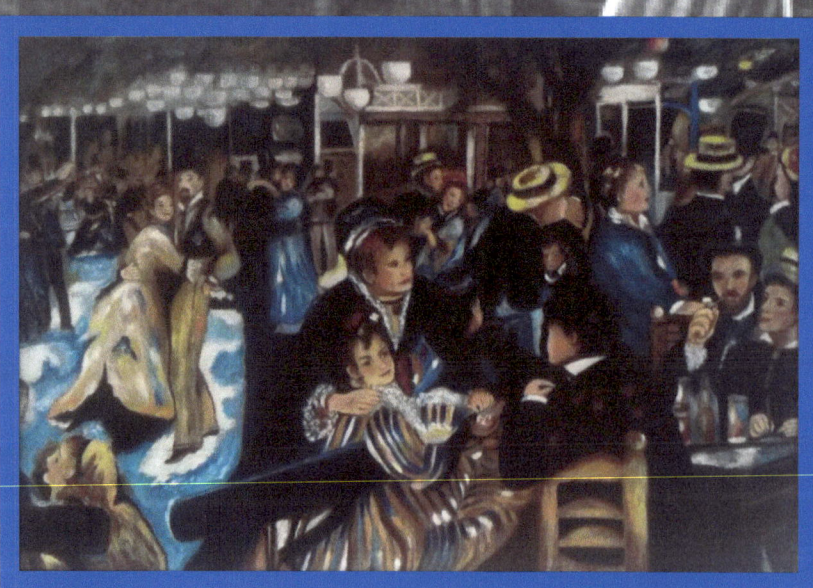

"Dance at Le Moulin de la Galette"

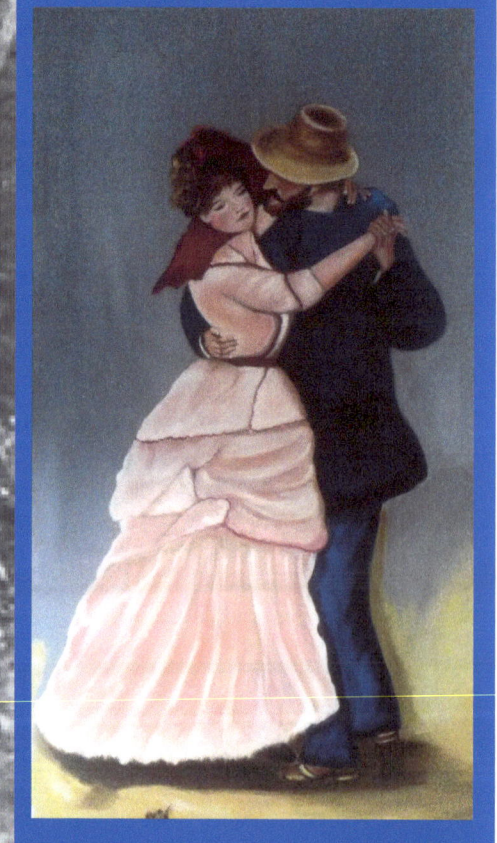

"Dance at Bougival"

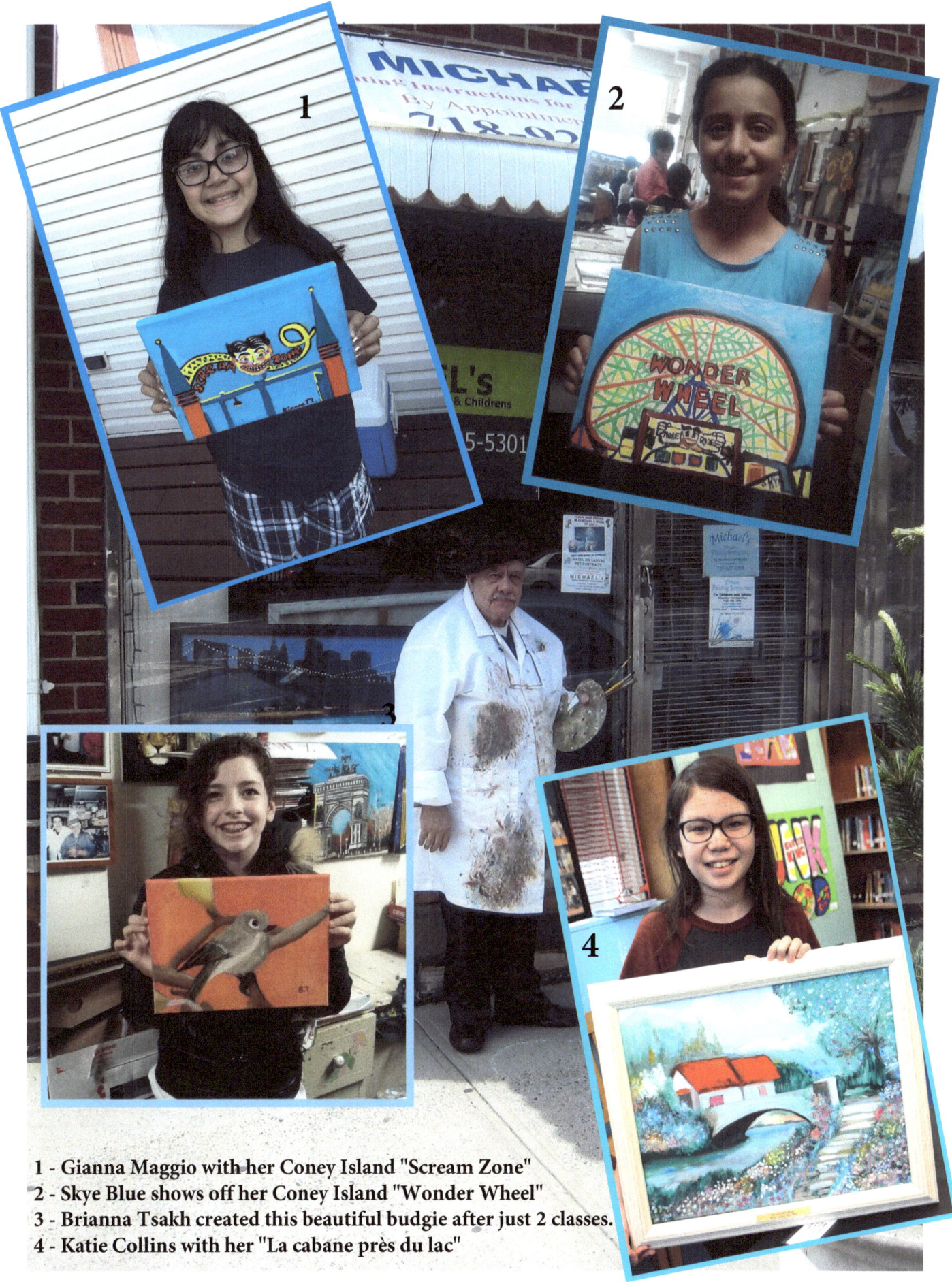

1 - Gianna Maggio with her Coney Island "Scream Zone"
2 - Skye Blue shows off her Coney Island "Wonder Wheel"
3 - Brianna Tsakh created this beautiful budgie after just 2 classes.
4 - Katie Collins with her "La cabane près du lac"

Globe Trotter

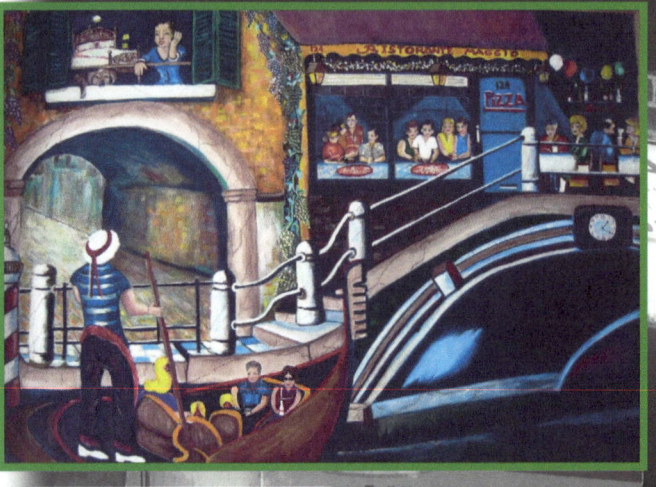

"Veni, Vici Venice!"
Oil on canvas

Michael has strayed far and wide away from his Bay Ridge studio and he's committed many of his global memories to canvas.

There is so much more that a painting or sketch can bring to a memory than a simple photograph can do.

A click of a button can capture an image on film or on a digital device but emotional strokes of a brush or the swirls of a pen or crayon add life to moments frozen in time.

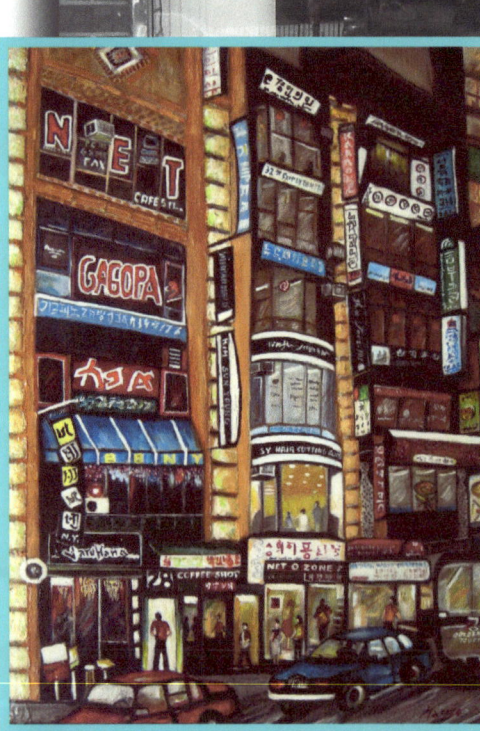

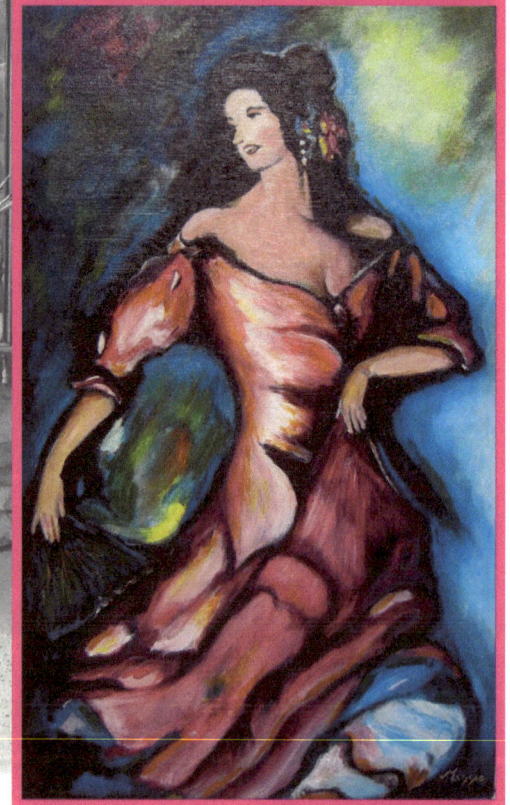

"A Taste of Korea in Manhattan"
Oil on canvas

"Flamenco!"
Oil on canvas

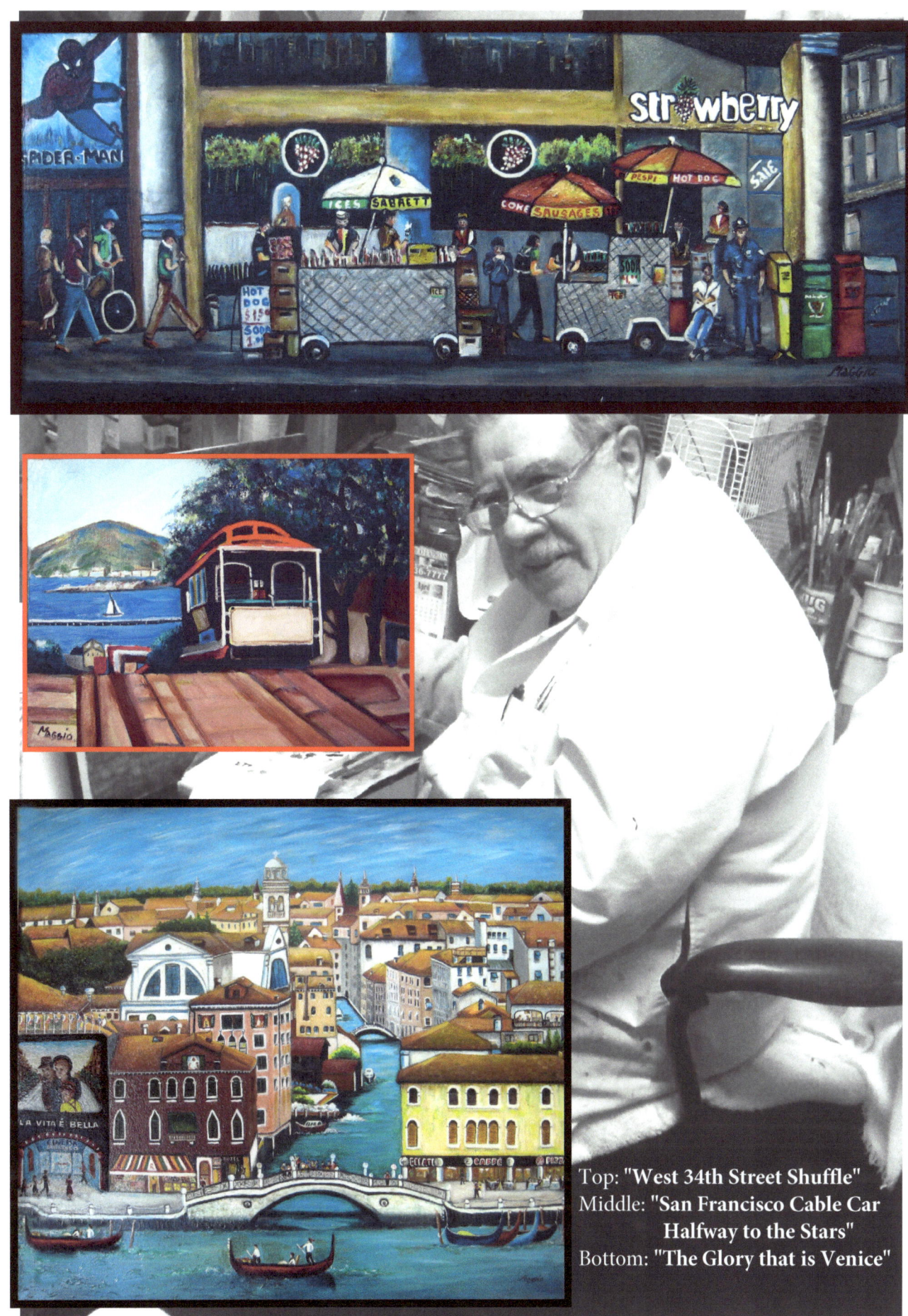

Top: "West 34th Street Shuffle"
Middle: "San Francisco Cable Car Halfway to the Stars"
Bottom: "The Glory that is Venice"

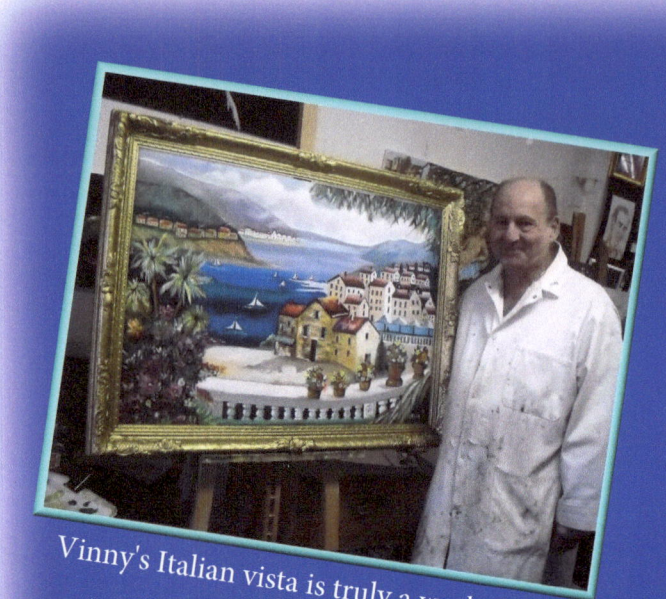

Vinny's Italian vista is truly a work of art.

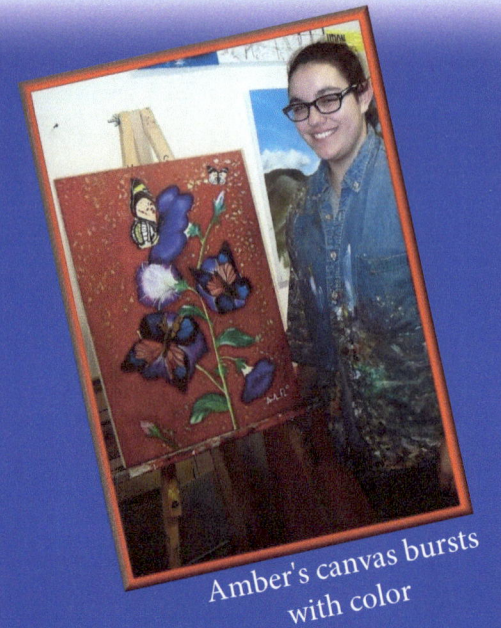

Amber's canvas bursts with color

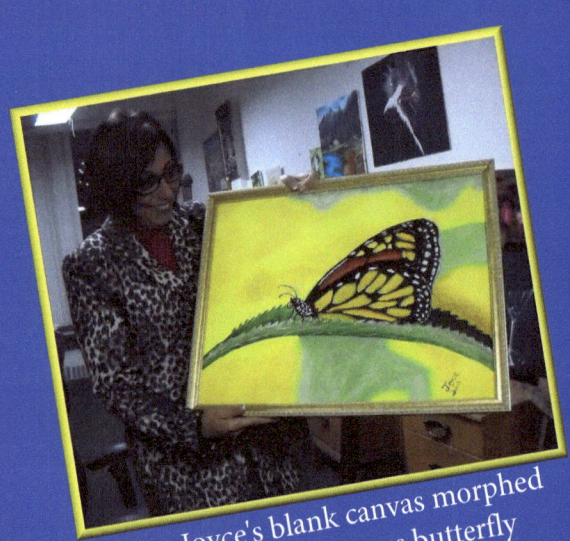

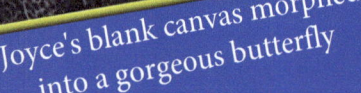

Joyce's blank canvas morphed into a gorgeous butterfly

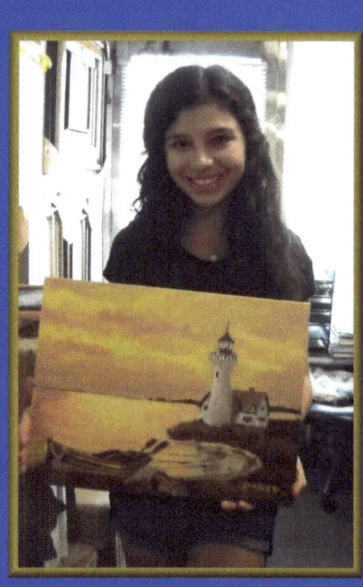

Carina created a spectacular scene

Kids have fun while learning at Michael's!

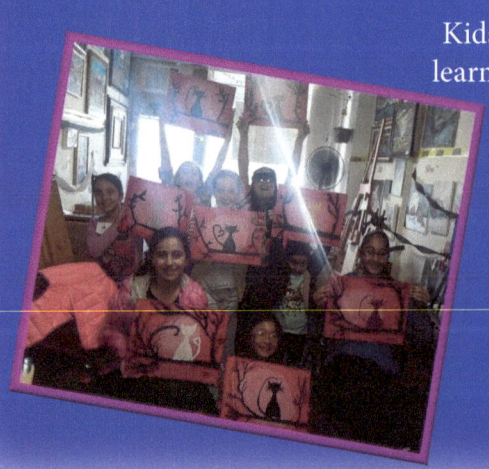

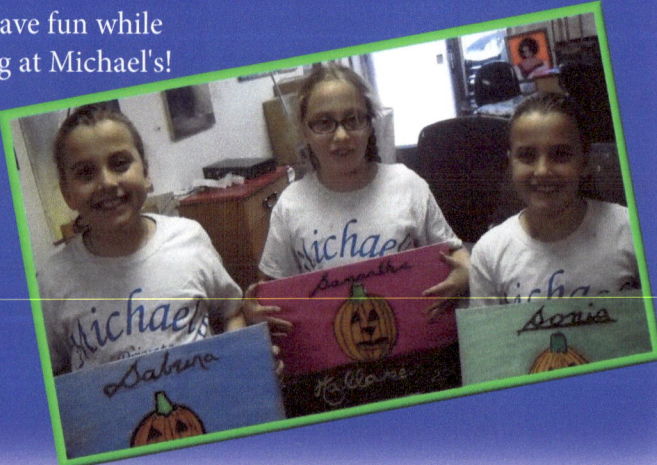

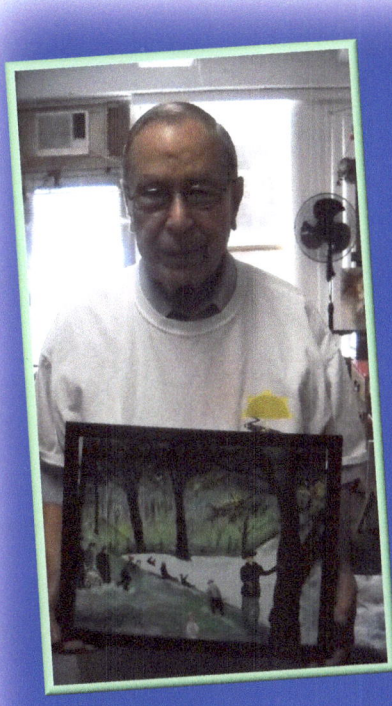

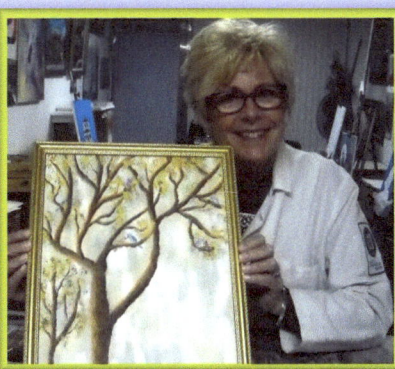

Diana's "Family Tree"

Mary Ann's gorgeous still life

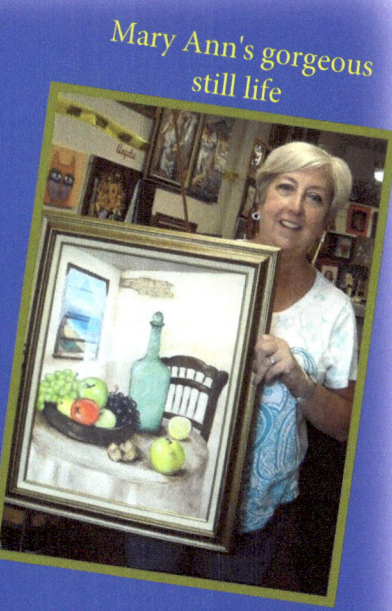

Dr. Gabriel's reminiscence of a New York Christmas from long ago.

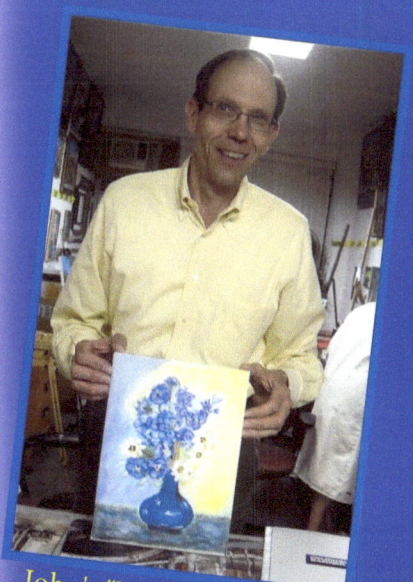

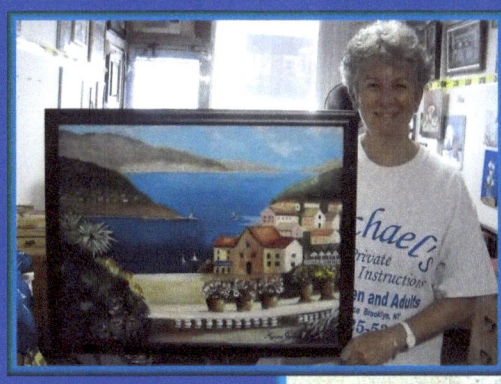

Marianne Sheehan creates another beautiful masterpiece and Michael captures her beauty in pastels on paper

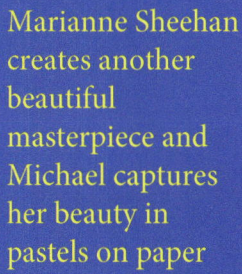

John's "budding" talent is obvious!

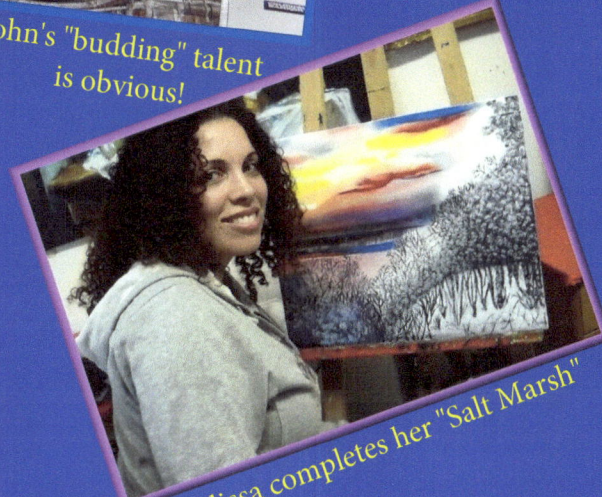

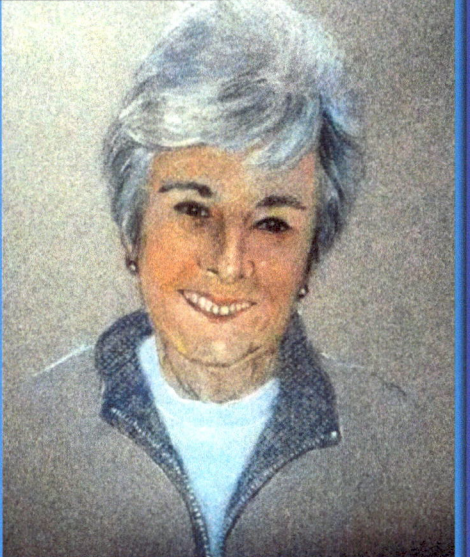

Melissa completes her "Salt Marsh"

37

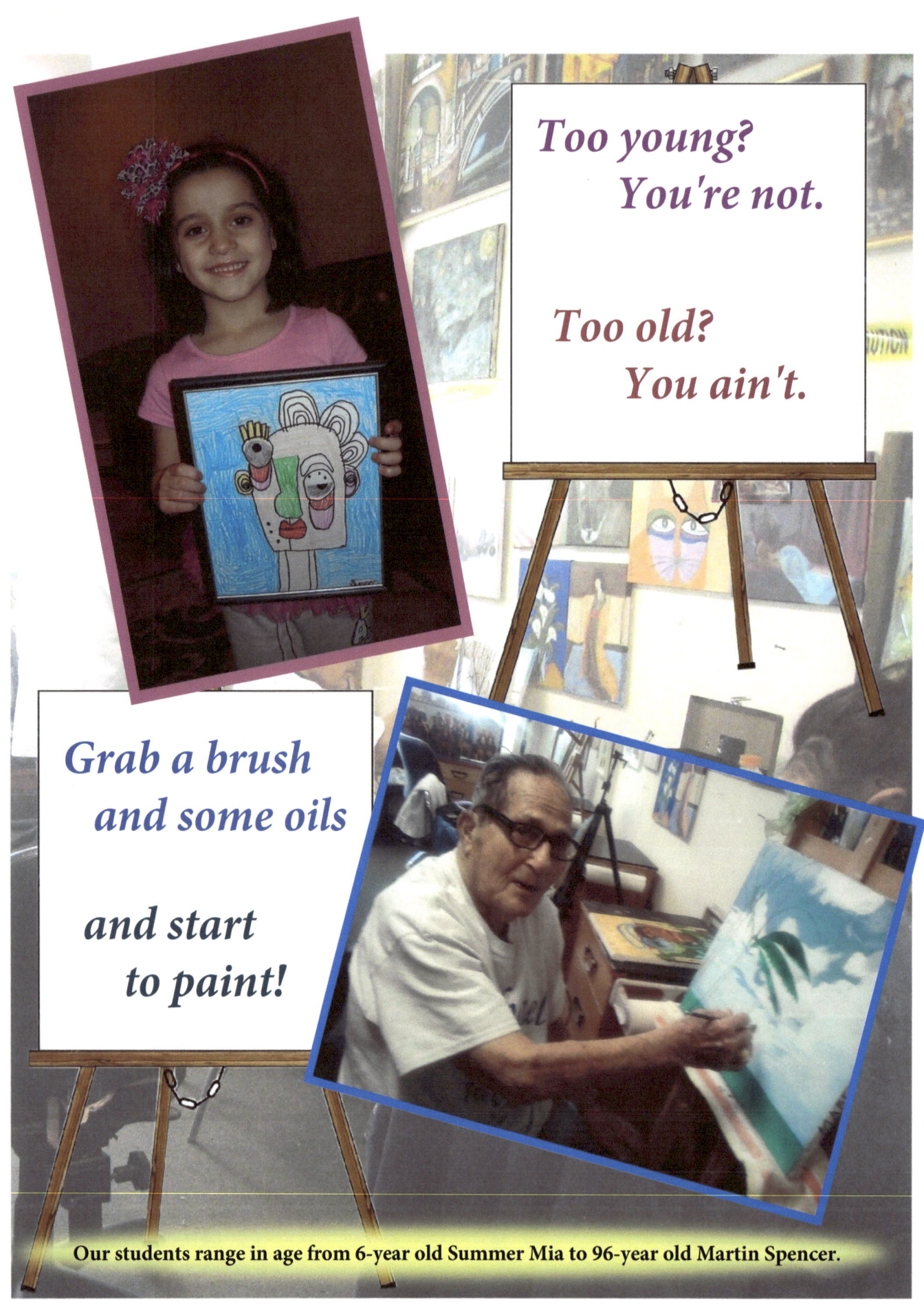

Too young?
You're not.

Too old?
You ain't.

Grab a brush
and some oils

and start
to paint!

Our students range in age from 6-year old Summer Mia to 96-year old Martin Spencer.

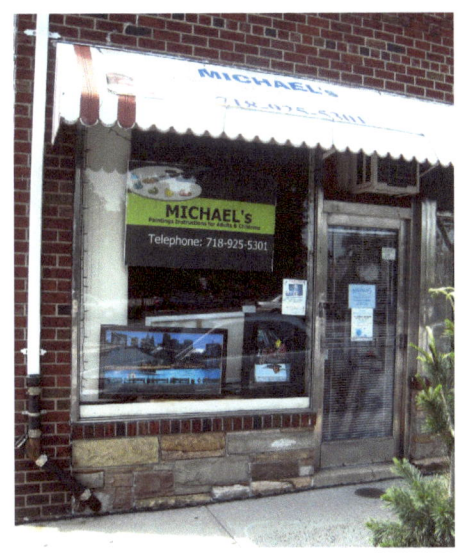

Hello, We Must Be Going

Thank you for the time you've invested in reading our first Art Annual from Michael's Painting Instructions.

If our images have encouraged you to take the time to relax in front of a canvas to express yourself, then we have succeeded. If our images and text have enticed you to visit our magnificent borough of Brooklyn, then we are here to welcome you.

We haven't meant to overstate the talents or results of any of our artists and no one at Michael's claims to be on par with the greats. We are just a group of like-minded art enthusiasts who love to paint and who love our town. All we want to do is share. Each and every one of us is, at best, a starving artist.

We look forward to our next annual in 2017 and we look forward to being in your hands again at that time.

If you are interested in viewing any of the art that has been shown herein, or should you wish to purchase or commission a personal piece of art in any medium, please don't hesitate to visit the studio on Parrot Place in Brooklyn, or to call Michael's Painting Instructions at 718-925-5301, or to email Michael directly at Maggio124@aol.com, or to visit our website at www.michaelspaintinginstructions .weebly.com

With a flourish of a brush stroke, we bid you good-bye until next year and, please, try to support your own local artists.

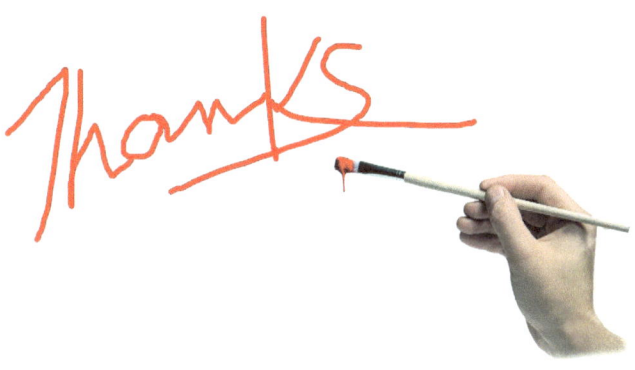

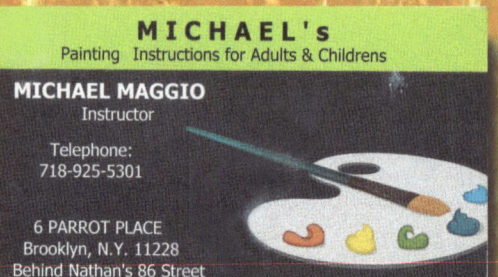
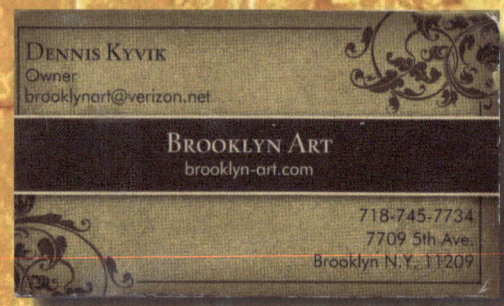
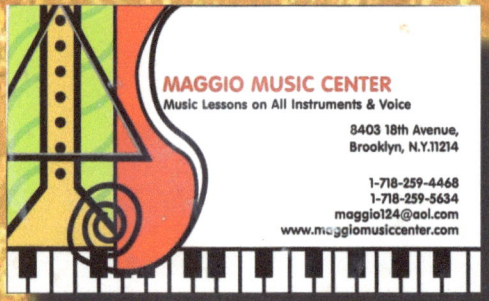
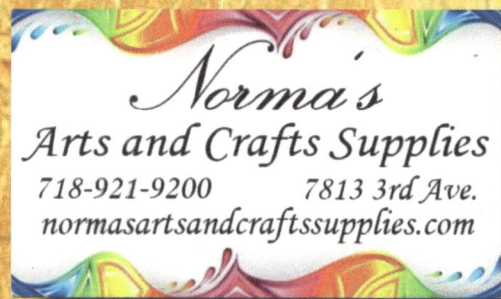
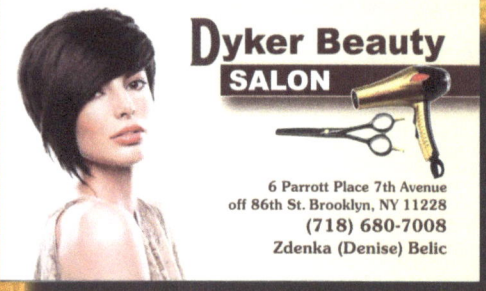
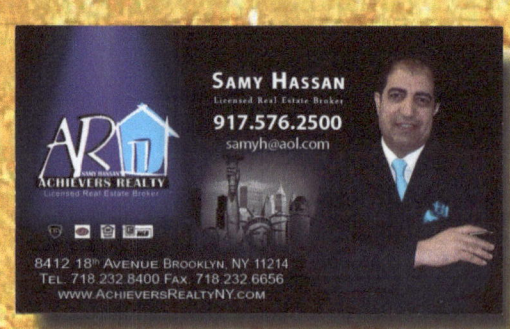
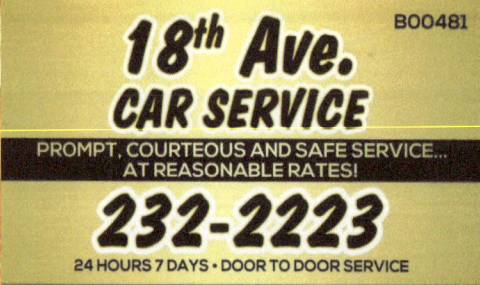

PLEASE SUPPORT BROOKLYN'S SPONSORS OF FINE ART

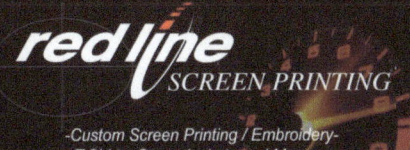
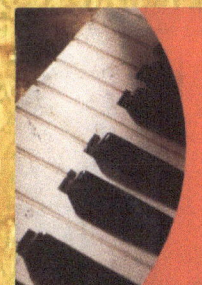
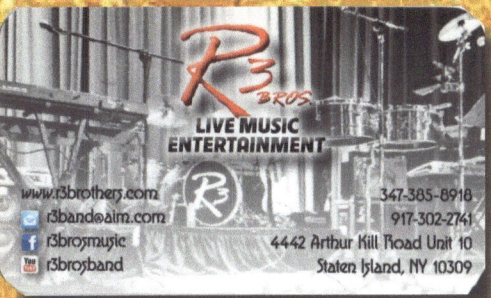
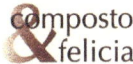

PLEASE SUPPORT BROOKLYN'S SPONSORS OF FINE ART

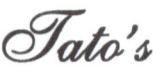
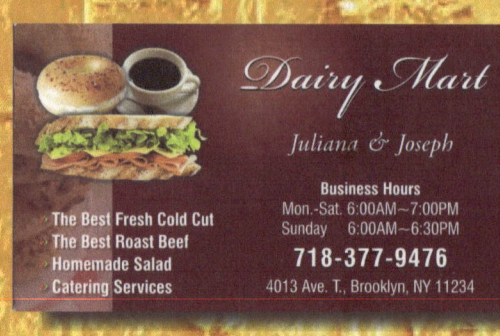
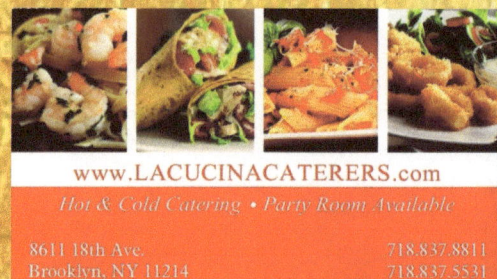
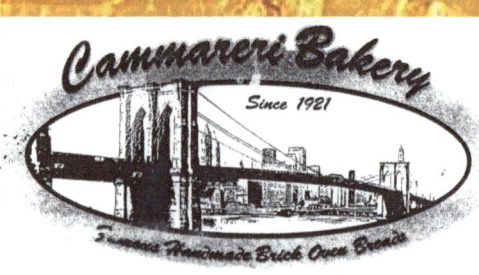
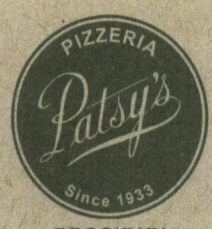

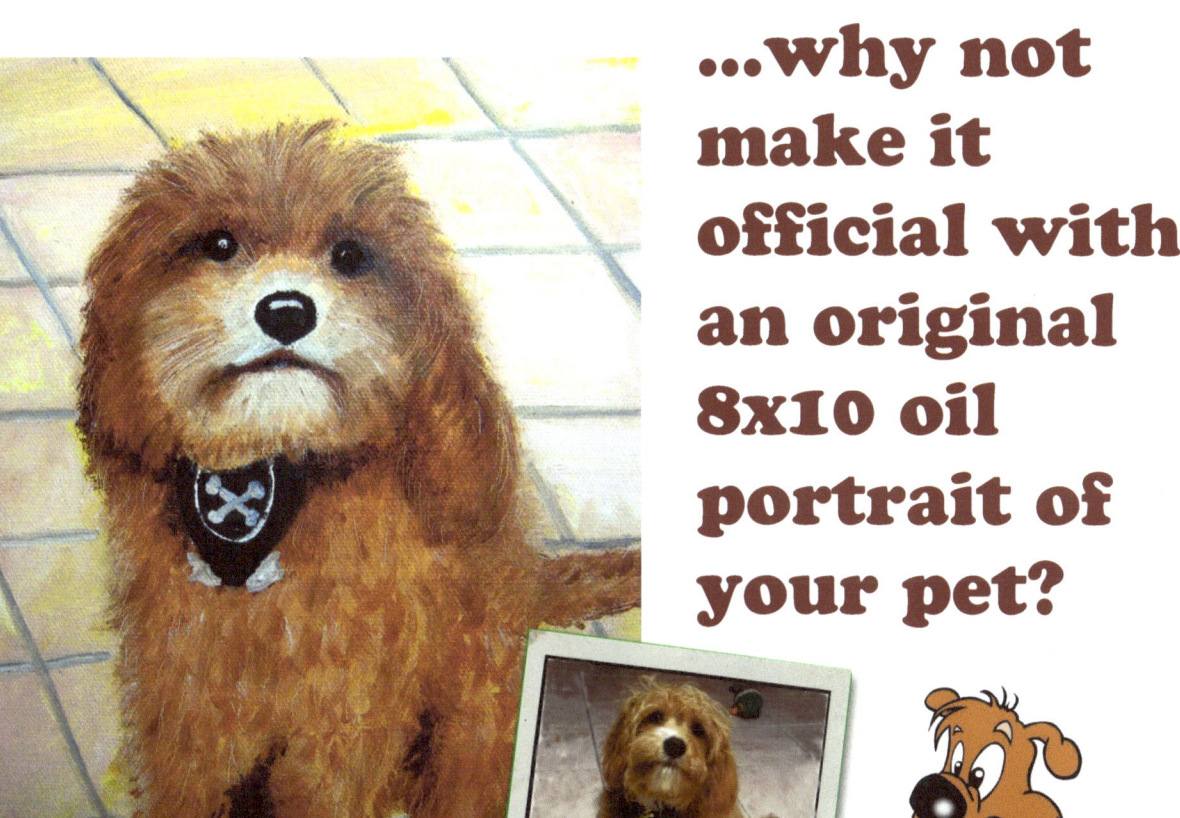

Brooklyn Remembers

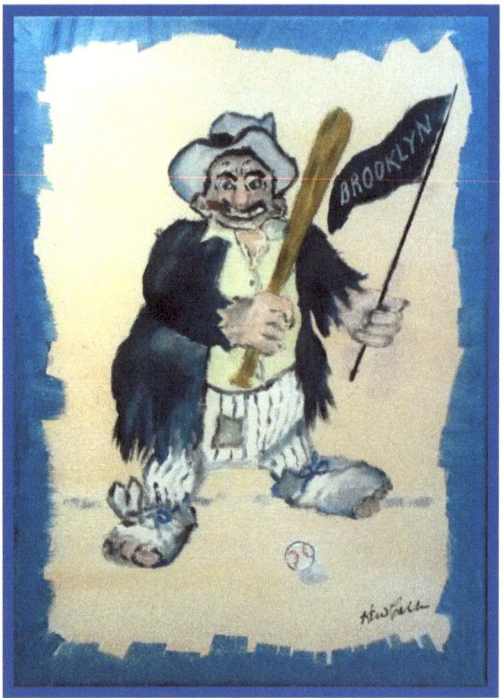

"A Loyal Bum" - Kevin Collins

Een Draght Mackt Maght

Brooklyn's Official Motto, from the Dutch: "In Unity Makes Strength"
often also written as "Eendraght Maeckt Maght"

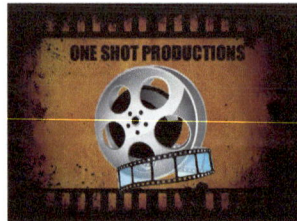

www.ingramcontent.com/pod-product-compliance
Lightning Source LLC
Chambersburg PA
CBHW040745200526

45159CB00023B/1738